RURAL AND REMOTE COMMUNITIES AS NON-STATE ACTORS

While entities as different as armed groups, multinational corporations, political parties, megacities, labour unions, terrorist organisations, or indigenous peoples are mentioned as non-state actors in the relevant literature, rural communities are never referred to. This book addresses the role of rural communities as non-state actors, lifting this invisibility veil with arguments coming from three theories of/scholarly approaches to international law: positivism, sociolegal realism (the New Haven School), and constitutionalism. It argues, first, that rural communities are recognised by the community of states as derived subjects of international law since they are made bearers of rights and duties in some major multilateral treaties. Second, rural communities have the ability to affect international lawmaking as they acquire the tools to influence decision-making in international arbitration and court litigation. Finally, the book highlights the need to recognise the status of rural communities when seeking global justice, as these are the communities that benefit the least from globalisation, while paying the highest price in terms of damage to the natural and sociocultural environment. Advocating for the existence of some supreme norms above the will of the states and the recognition of rural communities as non-state actors, this book will be of interest to academics, policy-makers, and non-governmental organisations working in the field of public international law and rural social matters.

Ciprian Nicolae Radavoi has a background in human rights law (lawyer in a firm with cases at the European Court of Human Rights) and diplomacy (consular positions in Northern Africa and Asia). Since 2012 he has taught international law and social justice subjects in China and in Australia and has published extensively on these matters.

David Price has researched and published widely on intellectual property protection in the Arabian Gulf States, including the intersection with international law and international trade. This extends to investor-state dispute settlement in the Gulf States, Indonesia, and Australia. He has worked in institutions in Australia, China, Europe, Indonesia, Oman, and the United Kingdom.

Routledge Research in International Law

Indigenous-Industry Agreements, Natural Resources and the Law
Edited by Ibironke T. Odumosu-Ayanu and Dwight Newman

Secession and Statehood
Lessons from Spain and Catalonia
Edited by Ana G Lopez and Jose Perea Unceta

The International Court of Justice and Municipal Courts
An Inter-Judicial Dialogue
Oktawian Kuc

Global Governance, Human Rights and International Law (2nd Edition)
Combating the Tragic Flaw
Errol P. Mendes

Small Island States and International Law
The Challenge of Rising Seas
Carolin König

Private International Law and Arbitral Jurisdiction
Faidon Varesis

Comparative and Transnational Dispute Resolution
Edited by Shahla Ali

Rural and Remote Communities as Non-State Actors
A Legal and Moral Argument
Ciprian Nicolae Radavoi and David Price

For more information about this series, please visit www.routledge.com/Routledge-Research-in-International-Law/book-series/INTNLLAW

Rural and Remote Communities as Non-State Actors
A Legal and Moral Argument

**Ciprian Nicolae Radavoi
and David Price**

LONDON AND NEW YORK

First published 2023
by Routledge
4 Park Square, Milton Park, Abingdon, Oxon OX14 4RN

and by Routledge
605 Third Avenue, New York, NY 10158

Routledge is an imprint of the Taylor & Francis Group, an informa business

© 2023 Ciprian Nicolae Radavoi and David Price

The right of Ciprian Nicolae Radavoi and David Price to be identified as authors of this work has been asserted in accordance with sections 77 and 78 of the Copyright, Designs and Patents Act 1988.

All rights reserved. No part of this book may be reprinted or reproduced or utilised in any form or by any electronic, mechanical, or other means, now known or hereafter invented, including photocopying and recording, or in any information storage or retrieval system, without permission in writing from the publishers.

Trademark notice: Product or corporate names may be trademarks or registered trademarks, and are used only for identification and explanation without intent to infringe.

British Library Cataloguing-in-Publication Data
A catalogue record for this book is available from the British Library

ISBN: 978-1-032-47263-8 (hbk)
ISBN: 978-1-032-47264-5 (pbk)
ISBN: 978-1-003-38531-8 (ebk)

DOI: 10.4324/9781003385318

Typeset in Times New Roman
by Apex CoVantage, LLC

Contents

Introduction   1

1   Developing Dialogues on the Non-State Actor Dynamic   7
Defining Non-State Actors 7
Non-State Actors in the Changing World 10
*Non-State Actors and the Russian Invasion
of Ukraine 11*
*The Individual as a Non-State Actor: New
Directions 14*
The Covid-19 Pandemic and Non-State Actors 17
*The Fourth Industrial Revolution and Non-State
Actors 18*

2   Rural Communities: Non-State Actors?   23
*The View From Positivism: Rural Communities in
International Law Regimes 23*
*The View From New Haven: Mobilised Rural
Communities in International Law 27*
*The View From Constitutionalism: Rural Communities'
Moral Standing 32*
*Taking the Argument Further: Remote Communities in
International Law 36*

Conclusion   45

Introduction

In January 2020, five tribal communities located in Louisiana and Alaska submitted a complaint to the United Nations (hereafter, UN), showing that the US government had failed to protect their human rights by allowing them to be forcibly displaced from their ancestral lands. They requested immediate intervention and investigation by the UN officials, in accordance with the UN Guiding Principles on Internal Displacement, the UN Declaration on the Rights of Indigenous Peoples, and other international human rights legal doctrine (Alaska Institute for Justice 2020). If a non-state actor is defined in international law as "an organized political actor not directly connected to the state but pursuing aims that affect vital state interests" (Pearlman and Cunningham 2012, 3), the complainant rural communities seem to qualify as non-state actors. They are organised political actors, they are remote and therefore very loosely connected with the US administrative and political structures, and they act on the international plane pursuing aims that affect vital state interests such as sovereignty, freedom from intervention in internal affairs, and international reputation.

Yet rural communities such as the five tribal communities referred to earlier are never mentioned in the burgeoning literature on non-state actors. Indeed, efforts to understand the extent to which non-state actors can fit conceptually into current understandings of international law have led to numerous books being published on the subject post-2000 (such as Arts, Noortmann, and Reinalda 2001; Alston 2005a; Clapham 2006; Noortmann, Reinisch, and Ryngaert 2015; Summers and Gough 2018; Scott et al. 2020), to a dedicated series at Routledge-Cavendish, and to the creation of a non-state actor–focussed academic journal in 2001, titled *Non-State Actors and International Law*. However, to the authors' knowledge, no publications have ever referred to rural communities as non-state actors. Academic works on non-state actors focus upon entities as diverse as intergovernmental organisations, multinational enterprises (MNEs), the Holy See, universities, mass media, rebel armed groups, the church, the International Olympic Committee and international sports federations, various other non-governmental organisations (NGOs), megacities, and even the individual—but not a word about

DOI: 10.4324/9781003385318-1

rural communities. Even an article that undertakes "to encourage exploration of the unlikely spaces where international law may indeed be found, but which are not visible on traditional 'maps' of international law" (Pearson 2008, 491) ignores villages and towns and sees cities only as an identifiable new space of international law.

This myopia may have to do with the absence of an operational and universally accepted definition of non-state actors. Broad definitions such as the one cited earlier reflect the difficulty of squeezing under the same conceptual roof the variety of entities listed as non-state actors in one publication or another. This is not too dissimilar to the difficulty encountered in the endeavour to define terrorism, when states could not agree on whether entities such as the armed forces of states and liberation movements should be included in the semantic sphere of the term. The solution, when the comprehensive counterterrorism convention proposed by India in 1996 could not advance because of this lack of definitional agreement, was to favour topical counterterrorism conventions, where the term could be defined in accordance with specific manifestations of terrorism, such as hijacking and bombing planes, taking hostages, and endangering maritime navigation. Similarly, defining non-state actors proves much easier when one considers the term's meaning as confined to a specific branch of international law: research in human rights, for example, builds definitions of non-state actors to match the characteristics of MNEs as possible bearers of human rights obligations, while scholarship in international humanitarian law looks at such entities as armed groups. Still, if the non-state actor concept is to retain real significance in international law theory and practice, an all-encompassing definition is needed.

One solution is to provide a broad general definition, combined with a non-limitative list of examples. For instance, the European Commission defines non-state actors as:

> a range of organisations that bring together the principal, existing or emerging, structures of the society outside the government and public administration. NSAs [non-state actors] are created voluntarily by citizens, their aim being to promote an issue or an interest, either general or specific. They are independent of the state and can be profit or non-profit-making organisations. The following are examples of NSAs: Non-Governmental Organisations/Community Based Organisations (NGO/CBO) and their representative platforms in different sectors, social partners (trade unions, employer associations), private sector associations and business organisations, associations of churches and confessional movements, universities, cultural associations, media.
>
> (European Commission 2002, 5)

The same approach has been employed by the International Law Association (ILA) which examined the issue at several of its biennial conferences, through the ILA's Committee on Non-State Actors, namely, the Rio (2008), Hague (2010), Sofia (2012), Washington (2014), and Johannesburg (2016) conferences. The Hague conference report clarified from the onset that the committee's understanding of a non-state actor was a functional one, defining non-state actors as "actors that actually perform functions in the international arena that have real or potential effects on international law" (ILA 2010, 6). It then added a list of exclusions (intergovernmental organisations, individuals, and such criminal organisations as the Mafia) and inclusions (NGOs with international legal status, MNEs, armed groups, indigenous peoples' groups etc.).

In its attempt to ascertain the reality of non-state actor practices, the Hague report (ILA 2010) further divided the domain of enquiry into *international lawmaking* by non-state actors on the one hand, and their *participatory rights* on the international plane on the other. Later on, the Johannesburg conference (2016) delivered the fourth and final report, which defined non-state actors as legally recognised and organised entities not controlled by the state and which actually perform functions with real and potential impacts on international law. This report admitted, however, that this working definition did not aspire to be shared by all scholars (ILA 2016, para. 19). Even though it represented the outcome of years of non-state actor examination at the ILA, the report also admitted the impracticability of squeezing them all into one category:

> NSAs play an important role in international practice that differs depending upon the particular actor and the area of activity. . . . Some NSAs have acquired formal legal personality, albeit a limited one, but others have not. Some take part in norm-creation and/or dispute settlement; others do not. Some have rights and duties, others do not. There is probably not a single legal characteristic that all NSAs share.
> (ILA 2016, para. 143)

The authors of the present book contend that this definitional haze—together with recent international dynamics that suggest the non-state actor definitional boundaries are now stretched further than ever before—permits, or perhaps requires, the inclusion of rural communities among the entities recognised as non-state actors. Chapter 1 crafts the foundations for this argument, first revisiting the boundaries of the definitional sphere to consider whether they could be conceived as including the rural community, and then noting developing dynamics (mainly, increasing impact and recognition of smaller actors in international law) that are congruent with some non-state actor role for the rural community.

Against this background, Chapter 2 then explores the hypothesis that *rural communities display enough of the characteristics required to be regarded as non-state actors*, specifically on the participatory (rather than lawmaking) side. Rural communities are neither specifically included in nor excluded from any of the non-limitative lists of non-state actors proposed in academia or by the ILA. They match the general definition in the sense that they are legally recognised, legitimate, organised entities. Admittedly, they are to some extent controlled by the state, which at first sight seems to place them outside the boundaries of the ILA definition. However, since cities are seen as non-state actors (Herrschel and Newman 2017; Aust and Nijman 2021), the 'state control' limitation appears to not apply to subnational administrative entities. The question that remains, therefore, is *whether rural communities perform functions with real and potential impacts on international law*.

The answer is complicated by the fact that the foundations of international law, like the foundations of law in general, have been conceived differently throughout the centuries. The foundation of law has chronologically been seen as either a value (natural law), a command of a power (positivism), or a norm generated within a social body and accepted as mandatory by its members (sociologism). Similarly, sense has been made of international law with a succession of meta-theories which, with the passing of time, have first replaced each other, but in the end they or their remnants or mutations have ended up coexisting: naturalism before the 19th century, positivism in the era of infant modern democracy, realism (a sociological theory) in the 20th century, and some form of naturalism again, in the form of constitutionalism (Orford and Hoffman 2016, 3–7).

Accordingly, Chapter 2 builds on Radavoi (2023) to answer the research question with a cautious "yes", with three different arguments, one developed in each of the three grand theories of international law—positivism, sociologism (realism), and naturalism. The first section of this chapter shows that in a framework of *international legal positivism*, rural communities are recognised by the community of states as 'derived' subjects of international law since they are made (directly, not via their state) bearers of rights and duties in some major multilateral treaties (Convention on Biological Diversity, Convention Concerning the Protection of the World Cultural and Natural Heritage, for example) and mentioned in soft law, such as Agenda 21. Further, some international law regimes are inherently referencing rural communities and thus seem favourably disposed to their recognition: an overwhelming proportion of indigenous peoples live in rural communities, as do members of the groups rebelling against the central authority in unstable countries.

The second section adopts the *realist views of the New Haven School*, which regards international law as embedded in the political context and analyses decision-making as blending patterns of authority and control. By analysing participants and their perspectives, their bases of power, strategies and so forth, New Haven scholars propose a set of tools to explain how various actors manage to influence international processes. In this perspective, it is relevant, for example, how rural communities mobilised against international investment have influenced decisions at the International Centre for Settlement of Investment Disputes (ICSID), or how compensation claims brought against MNEs by villagers in developing countries have been successful in the home country's courts. The key word of the second section is mobilisation.

Finally, the third section proposes a view from *constitutionalism*, the theory that integrates state and non-state actors in a broader concept of global constitutional community. From a normative standpoint, a necessary feature of constitutionalisation is the participation of affected individuals in decision-making. People in rural communities are most affected by water pollution, climate change (for example, desertification, sea level rise), or nuclear waste dumping—yet they do not have a voice. While less affected, urban populations are somehow more able to avail themselves of the protections of international law; in fact, there is now an important current in international law theory accepting that cities are non-state actors.

Once having established that rural communities can be seen as non-state actors, the stakes are further raised in the last section, where it is argued that not only rural communities generally, but also the subset of them known as remote communities display characteristics of non-state actors.

References

Alaska Institute for Justice. 2020. *Rights of Indigenous People in Addressing Climate-Forced Displacement*. Complaint Submitted to the United Nations, January 1, 15. https://s3.documentcloud.org/documents/6656724/Louisiana-Tribes-Complaint-to-UN.pdf.

Alston, Philippe, ed. 2005a. *Non-State Actors and Human Rights*. Oxford: Oxford University Press.

Arts, Bas, Math Noortmann, and Bob Reinalda. 2001. *Non-State Actors in International Relations*. Burlington: Ashgate.

Aust, Helmut P., and Janne E. Nijman, eds. 2021. *Research Handbook on International Law and Cities*. Cheltenham: Edward Elgar.

Clapham, Andrew. 2006. *Human Rights Obligations of Non-State Actors*. Oxford: Oxford University Press.

European Commission. 2002. *Communication from the Commission to the Council, the European Parliament and the Economic and Social Committee: Participation of Non-State Actors in EC Development Policy*. COM (2002) 598 final.

Herrschel, Tassilo, and Peter Newman. 2017. *Cities as International Actors: Urban and Regional Governance Beyond the Nation State*. London: Palgrave MacMillan.

International Law Association (ILA). 2010. "Non-State Actors." Report, The Hague Conference.

———. 2012. "Non-State Actors in International Law: Lawmaking and Participation Rights." Report, Sofia Conference.

———. 2016. "Non-State Actors." Final Report, Johannesburg Conference.

Noortmann, Math, August Reinisch, and Cedric Ryngaert, eds. 2015. *Non-State Actors in International Law*. Oxford: Hart Publishing.

Orford, Anne, and Florian Hoffman. 2016. "Introduction: Theorizing International Law." In *The Oxford Handbook of the Theory of International Law*, edited by Anne Orford and Florian Hoffman, 1–18. Oxford: Oxford University Press.

Pearlman, Wendy, and Kathleen Cunningham. 2012. "Nonstate Actors, Fragmentation, and Conflict Processes." *Journal of Conflict Resolution* 56 (1): 3–15.
Pearson, Zoe. 2008. "Spaces of International Law." *Griffith Law Review* 17 (2): 489–514.
Radavoi, Ciprian N. 2023. "Rural Communities in International Law: Non-State Actors?" *Texas International Law Journal* 58 (1): 1–19.
Scott, Karen N., Kathleen Claussen, Charles-Emmanuel Côté, and Atsuko Kanehara. 2020. *Changing Actors in International Law*. Leiden: Brill.
Summers, James, and Alex Gough, eds. 2018. *Non-State Actors and International Obligations: Creation, Evolution and Enforcement*. Boston and Leiden: Brill.

1 Developing Dialogues on the Non-State Actor Dynamic

Defining Non-State Actors

For decades, the question of what might or should constitute a non-state actor has preoccupied the minds of international law scholars. What is its essential qualification—state acknowledgement, acquired legal personality, power, function, outcome? Organisation, size, or some/most of the preceding? Despite a recent proliferation of literature on non-state actors and their roles in governance and development, alluded to in the Introduction, there is relatively little consensus about the nature of a non-state actor.

What is noticeable, however, is the development over time of a hierarchy of terms and descriptors that builds complexity. The simple earlier descriptors tend to explain non-state actors in terms of what they are not, namely, not a state actor. This negative form of description is not particularly helpful, but one sees advances with the umbrella form of generalisation to which qualifiers add distinction, and then an inclusive approach compiled by exemplars. The negative form might state, for example, that non-state actors are not "bodies comprised of and governed or controlled by States or groups of States" (ILA 2010).

Alston (2005b, 3) asserted that these negative, euphemistic terms did not stem from language inadequacies but instead had been intentionally adopted in order to reinforce the assumption that the state is not only the central actor but also the indispensable and pivotal one around which all other entities revolve. He lamented that this insistence upon defining actors in terms of what they are not combines impeccable purism in terms of traditional international legal analysis with an unparalleled capacity to marginalise a significant part of the international human rights regime from the most vital challenges confronting global governance at the dawn of the 21st century.

With the addition of certain qualifiers or notations of action or area activity, substance was added to the skeleton definition. The additions are not necessarily unanimous or consistent, and they can include:

- "all those actors that are not (representatives of) states, yet that operate at the international level and are potentially relevant to international relations" (Arts 2003, 5; emphasis added)

DOI: 10.4324/9781003385318-2

- "legally recognized and organised entities that are not comprised of nor governed or controlled by States nor groups of States and that actually perform functions in the international arena that have real or potential effects on international law" (ILA 2016, para. 19; emphasis added)

These descriptions may appear similar but still demonstrate differing key normative and operational distinctions. It could be said that the first implies some form of legal relationship with a state actor or actors by being required to be relevant to international relations. The second description implies a specific role—"performs functions"—but also implies the requirement of some form of legal personality by having the capacity to influence international law. Arts, presenter of the first above definition, would most likely disagree with the distinction between the two as being trivial or non-existent since both descriptors include the core element of a non-state actor of power (Arts 2003, 4). The difference, however, is important and may be a reflection of progress in non-state actor theory in the time that elapsed between the two definitions.

Progress on the one hand meant simply raising the definitional threshold, from an entity that is merely "relevant to international relations" (Arts 2003, 5) to one "pursuing aims that affect vital state interests" (Pearlman and Cunningham 2012, 3). But it also meant clarification by atomisation when authors (for example, Worster 2016) suggested to retire the notion of the monolithic, singular status of the international legal person—anything that is "potentially relevant to international relations" or "affects vital state interests", as in the previously quoted definitions—and instead recognise that personality is essentially a status of holding rights and duties, and that rights and duties fluctuate based on functions. States might still be placed in a special category as the grantors of rights, but there needs to be acknowledgement that other entities are increasingly enjoying relative personality based on their functions.

The function-based approach leads to definitional offerings adding useful detail but becoming constrained by the context or theme of the work in which the respective non-state actor is presented. The Cotonou Agreement, for example, signed in 2000 between the European Union and the African, Caribbean, and Pacific group of states with the aim of eradicating poverty, referred to non-state actors as "private sector, economic and social partners, including trade union organisations, civil society in all its forms according to national characteristics". When the discussion is on international policymaking, Nasiritousi, Hjerpe, and Bäckstrand (2016, 939) refer to non-state actors as "any group participating in global governance that is not a sovereign state, while excluding armed and criminal groups"; obviously, no one wants terrorists or the Mafia at the table when devising international policy. Finally, when the subject of scrutiny is the functioning of areas of limited statehood, non-state actors are "actors that are not part of the internationally and nationally recognised sovereign state but exert notable influence (whether positive or negative) on the functioning of the state [including] community-based and civil society groups, humanitarian and development organisations, armed actors and opposition groups, and the private sector and business interests, all working at various levels" (Perera 2015).

So at this stage, there exist reasonably detailed area-specific definitions of non-state actors but only very vague general definitions, not far above the 'not-a-state' level of precision. The challenges confronting commentators and experts in reaching general consensus on accurately characterising their nature and role are highlighted by the Report of the Committee of the International Law Association on Non-state Actors, and ILA's response to the report. Researched and developed over almost a decade, the report elaborates as much on points of divergence as on points of consensus. Delivered and adopted at the ILA's international conference in 2016, the final report provides a rich source of material in the ongoing debate on the nature and scope of non-state actors. The report defines them as "legally recognized and organised entities that are not comprised of nor governed or controlled by States nor groups of States and that actually perform functions in the international arena that have real or potential effects on international law" (ILA 2016, para. 19). However, it immediately recognises the inbuilt shortcomings of the definition by acknowledging that it is only a working, operational one which might not, and which does not aspire to, be shared by all scholars.

The report then adds some examples of non-state actors, namely, the conventional list of non-governmental and community-based organisations and their representative platforms in different sectors, social partners (trade unions, employer associations), private sector associations and business organisations, associations of churches and confessional movements, universities, cultural associations, and media. The commission continues that non-state actors are either operational or advocates. The tradition so far in European Commission cooperation with non-state actors was to support them when they came to provide services in sensitive fields and implement projects to cover the basic needs of vulnerable groups in socially or geographically isolated areas. In most developing countries, non-state actors are also increasingly becoming advocates, by taking part in consultation processes with external donors and in policy discussions and by contributing to the definition of their countries' strategies, thereby advancing ownership of the development process as well as deepening democracy and increasing accountability of both the state and the business sector. Non-state actors often constitute the decisive operational element in public/private partnerships, including those partnerships on research and technological development.

The ILA, in validating the work of its committee in 2016, signalled the need for further exploration of some issues raised by the 2016 report. It acknowledged the fact that the committee had adopted a broad working definition of non-state actors but that it was not possible to draw general or particular conclusions without more specific analysis of individual types of non-state actors. Finally, it recognised a corresponding need for an applied typology of non-state actors and a differentiated examination of the status, rights, and/or duties of specific types of non-state actors under international law.

The fundamental question, from this book's perspective, is how such rights and duties are attained when it comes to the rural community. For non-state actors in general, they often arise directly from function, as in the case of intergovernmental organisations (IGOs), international non-governmental organisations (INGOs), or multinational enterprises (MNEs) (Worster 2016; ILA 2016). In this perspective, the numerous international treaties assigning roles to rural communities in pursuance of the respective treaty's scope (see Chapter 2, 'The View From Positivism: Rural Communities in International Law Regimes') speak in favour of accepting a (limited) non-state actor role for those communities.

But the relevant rights and duties could also be in part informed by the degree of influence or powers of persuasion that an entity striving to be acknowledged as a non-state actor can bring to bear on others to notice, support, act upon, or even oppose and denounce the issue or issues put forward by that putative non-state actor. When, for example, the protests of a mobilised rural community lead to the unilateral termination by the host state of an international investment contract, this invites reflection on rights and duties under international law. Admittedly, such a position does not sit comfortably with the traditional rules relating to legal personality. But as shown earlier, the contemporary understanding of the non-state actor sees it as nothing more than "an active participant in the international legal process, as opposed to a mere spectator" (Côté 2020, 10); the attraction of the generic term 'actor' is, as Côté shows, exactly the fact that it eludes the more complex question of the specific non-state actor's legal status. With the changing nature of the global society and events over the last decade in particular—including those examined in the following section—entities that used to be mere spectators assert or are about to assert participative roles on the international stage.

Non-State Actors in the Changing World

The current dynamics of the global society and international law as driven by current international politics should add further energy to the current debate on the nature of transnational non-state actors. This section considers four current developments, both short and long term, with international impact and in which non-state actors are actively involved: (a) the Russian invasion of Ukraine and the participation of many non-state actors; (b) new manifestations of the individual as a non-state actor; (c) the Covid-19 pandemic and the reaffirmation of the state; and (d) the emergence of the 'fourth industrial revolution' and new technologies. These four developments are both exemplars and creators of complications in respect of the expanding compendium of established non-state actor characteristics. They may cause some newcomers to be elevated in status while causing others to be reduced in status or even discarded. A brief overview of each, through these lenses, serves the purpose of this book by showing that the list of non-state actors is not immutable.

Non-State Actors and the Russian Invasion of Ukraine

What has already become remarkable with the Russian invasion of Ukraine is the number of discrete actors involved in what, in its simplest trite expression, is essentially a territorial sovereignty dispute between two neighbouring states. There are the two state actors in open combat, other state actors providing material and humanitarian support for the invaded combatant, and yet other state actors providing material support for the invading combatant. Further, there are state actors declaring a position of non-participation with limited trade relations, while further state actors declare a neutral position but on occasion offer an intermediary role. Established IGOs, INGOs, NGOs, MNEs, and a host of other civil society organisations have pursued refugee, humanitarian, and human rights support and assistance to the combat zone and displaced civil populations. Another host of non-state actors, some not recognised or even identified, have become involved in the conflict in a range of non-combatant roles, as summarised later in this section. At the same time, armed non-state actors are actively involved in some of the harshest fighting: the Wagner Group and other mercenaries on the Russian side, and international battalions, foreign fighters, and military advisers within Ukrainian regular forces.

The Russian annexation of Crimea in 2014 and the current invasion in the east, with missile attacks on the capital Kyiv and other main centres in the country, is tending to overturn the comfortable and established views of the parameters and definitions of international law and the constituent elements identifying state actors and the various established categories of non-state actors. Li (2022) asserts that various non-state actors have played important roles of disruption in the conflict and complicated interactions with traditional state actors. Prominent international capitalists, small and medium-sized technological entities, and emerging international platforms have all taken advantage of their own strengths to get involved in the conflict as well as the corresponding diplomatic games.

Writing at the very start of the Russian invasion of Ukraine, Rosenblat (2022) commented on the millions of people rallying in Ukraine and around the world in support of democracy generally and Ukraine specifically. She suggested that, while a flood of economic and diplomatic sanctions from Western governments may raise the cost of Putin's invasion, it would be the pressure from Russian grassroots civil society, business leaders, and transnational advocacy networks that would to a large extent determine Ukraine's fate (Rosenblat 2022, 160). Indeed, 1 year (at the time of this writing) after the Russian invasion commenced, Ukraine continues to repel the invaders and even recover some territory lost in the early months of fighting.

Their success has in large part been achieved by the massive contributions of moral support and material assistance in the form of military hardware and humanitarian immediate and longer-term aid and assistance. The range of support encompasses state actors but also almost the whole panoply of organisations and groups already recognised as non-state actors—as well as a host of new and emerging groups and individuals. Together, they will test the current parameters of who/what constitute a non-state actor at a time of transnational armed conflict. Notably, the contributions so far have been of national, international, and transnational sources; they have encompassed both ends of the conflict scale—in the interests of armed conflict and then in the interests of humanitarian welfare, emergency aid, and human rights of the victims.

Over the past few decades, non-state actors have played significant roles in the international community, yet there have been few cases where they were so directly and prominently involved in significant international affairs as in the case of the current war. Indeed, their intervention in the Russia–Ukraine conflict has significantly expanded the combat space. Most of the non-state actor activity has undoubtedly been in support of the Ukrainian cause, even allowing for the probability that much is still not in the public domain. In the field of combat, the Ukrainian forces have been bolstered by volunteers from expatriate and diaspora sources. Fighters from the United Kingdom and other European countries, the United States, Canada, Japan, and other countries, many of whom have had military experience, have volunteered to fight alongside Ukrainian forces in the International Legion under the Ukraine military command. Formally known as the 'International Legion of Territorial Defence of Ukraine', the international legion contains a number of loose nationality-based brigades, with volunteers coming from 60 different countries (Chan 2022).

The Ukrainian campaign has also benefited significantly from a virtual army of technology companies and individual specialists undertaking a campaign against Russian computer, social media, and IT-based systems. The support has been in both hardware and software and IT support and has incorporated the far superior capabilities of Western states and commercial operatives. The support has included both hacking Russian government, financial, and commercial systems and protecting Ukraine's systems from Russian cyberattacks. Belarus systems have also been targeted. The hacking group known as Anonymous issued a call on social media for hackers all over the globe to launch a cyberwar against Russia, and more than 1,500 websites related to Russian and Belarusian governments, media, banks, and companies have been attacked (Li 2022). A UK company has been providing military-grade satellite imagery of Russian-held territory. Such social media websites as Twitter and Facebook have taken restrictive measures against Russian media, prohibiting them from publishing ads or monetising their content.

On the corporate side, many businesses have dramatically downsized their Russian operations, reduced supply chains, or closed down entirely. Boeing and Airbus have ceased providing parts for the Russian aviation industry, while major companies such as McDonalds and Starbucks have withdrawn from the country and closed down their operations entirely. Elon Musk publicly threw his support behind Ukraine and committed to maintain his Starlink satellite system, a public access internet system and, more importantly, a crucial weapon in the drone campaign by both the military and non-state actors (volunteers) to locate and track Russian positions, artillery and missile sites, and troop and supply movements (Li 2022).

The Ukraine funding tracker organisation Devex records that its Funding Platform tracks more than 850 sources of information about the largest funders around the world, including national governments, multilateral agencies, and the biggest philanthropic foundations (Ainsworth 2023). Its database reveals over $50 billion worth of grants and other contributions. The funding is primarily for humanitarian activity and to maintain essential infrastructure in Ukraine, and the figure more than doubled between October and December 2022.

In the community, citizen groups have reported Russian military activity, including using drone technology to do so; funded or purchased military equipment such as uniforms, winter clothing, and flak jackets for Ukrainian forces; gathered or preserved evidence of alleged Russian atrocities (mostly committed in rural communities!) for possible future war crimes investigations and prosecutions; and donated cryptocurrencies to the government. On the other side, reports have emerged of the Ukrainian Secret Service uncovering and dismantling a pro-Russian network of individuals and teams within Ukraine that were providing intelligence to the Russian military command on the coordinates of Ukrainian critical infrastructure facilities, including energy infrastructure, and Ukrainian air defence systems locations (Vavra 2023).

In terms of armed non-state actors, the private military company known as 'the Wagner Group' has made a significant contribution to Russia's military capacity. Well-trained and armed, and with a high standard of combat experience from participation in conflict campaigns elsewhere, they have largely been at the forefront of Russian successes in the battlefield. Although in close contact with regular frontline forces operationally, and despite their founder Yevgeny Prigozhin being part of President Putin's inner circle, Russian officials have refuted claims that they are embedded into the military command and organisational structure. Accordingly, and since they have the capacity to operate independently, they would constitute a non-state actor, notwithstanding that a post-conflict tribunal would likely hold that their military activities may be attributable to the state. A number of media outlets have regularly reported on the Wagner Group actively recruiting Russians and pro-Russian sympathisers abroad (notably from central Asia) to their frontline forces.

It has also been recruiting, allegedly forced, within the Russian prison system with the approval and cooperation of the Russian authorities (Ziener and King 2022).

Beyond the direct military conflict, and from its very beginning, Russia was reportedly establishing networks operating in major international financial centres to enable it to continue trading in currencies and stock markets and recruiting legal and public relations firms specifically for the purpose of promoting its cause. Compliant multiple encrypted currency platforms including Binance and Coinbase are reportedly refusing to enforce an all-around ban on Russian clients, claiming that excluding the entire country would be inconsistent with Bitcoin's spirit of providing payment channels free of government oversight and having a significant ameliorating effect on Western financial sanctions against Russia (Li 2022). And it appears that Russian oligarchs are required to utilise their wealth and international trade and political connections and networks to contribute to the maintenance of deteriorating Russian trade relations and to facilitate new trade opportunities in the face of Western-imposed sanctions—notwithstanding the consequences of being individually listed and sanctioned and of seizure of assets (Schmidt and Carpenter 2022). They are also required/expected to add their weight to the Russian propaganda machinery to legitimise the legitimacy of the Russian campaign. Failure to do so appears to run the risk of meeting unfortunate fatal accidents.

The outcome of the Russian–Ukraine war is still uncertain, and arguably largely dependent on the determination of Western state actors that a Russian victory will not be tolerated. More likely outcomes, then, may be a reclaim by Ukraine of at least some of its sovereign territory, either via combat or a negotiated peace, possibly with a post-Putin regime. But whatever its eventual outcome, the Russian–Ukraine war will quite possibly change the face of European geopolitics, and the character of a wide range of state and non-state actors. Indeed, as Li (2022) explains, with their intervention in the Russia–Ukraine conflict as a hallmark, non-state actors are demonstrating a new momentum. Their rhetorical impacts and actual influence have risen further, and they have dealt prominent blows to the pattern of international relations dominated by state actors. The continuous development of non-state actors will inevitably change the interactive factors in international relations, thus becoming an important force affecting the evolution of the international order.

The Individual as a Non-State Actor: New Directions

The aftermath of World War II brought about a strong affirmation of the individual's role in international law, as bearer of both rights and obligations, thus limiting the century-old doctrine of Westphalian sovereignty which had largely obscured, for centuries, the role of individual in international law. In terms of rights, the Universal Declaration of Human Rights adopted in 1948 laid the foundations for the two International Covenants (of civil and political, and of social economic and cultural rights, respectively) adopted in 1966, and subsequently the complex architecture of regional and topical human rights treaties, some of which afford to the individual judicial avenues of complaint against their own state, in the international law (most reputably, the European Court of Human Rights). Another example of procedural avenues for the individual to defend rights against states in international law is offered by the international investment regime, with its investor-state dispute resolution system. In terms of obligations, the role of the individual as a non-state actor has been demonstrated by the post–World War II International Military Tribunals at Nuremberg and Tokyo; the United Nations (UN) tribunals for Yugoslavia and Rwanda; tribunals and special courts in Sierra Leone, Lebanon, Cambodia, and Timor-Leste; and finally the adoption of the International Criminal Court statute in 1998. The affirmation of both rights and obligations, being sanctioned with procedural capacities for individuals in international courts, seems to establish without doubt their status as non-state actors.

However, beyond the clear-cut examples of armed criminal activity and preservation of human rights, the status of individual personality becomes contentious. The Committee of the ILA specifically limited the types of actors included in its research on the nature of non-state actors to those that were internationally legally recognised and organised entities. Thus, individuals were expressly excluded because they were not "organised entities" (ILA 2010, 6)—a limitation dictated by the functionalist approach, since individuals generally do not fulfil functions related to international law. Accordingly, Worster (2016, 269), in line with the functionalist approach, suggests that questions are now being raised regarding whether every individual has some capacity for international personality. He concludes that the existence and degree of international legal personality in individuals are fluctuating and relative, depending on the state of international law and the needs of the international community, which potentially keeps the door open for future expansion of personality.

To Worster's functionality, it is suggested that influence could be added—that is, influence by traditional non-state actors, but also by private individuals who become drivers of international political change, or who stimulate other (state and non-state) actors to influence events with impact on international law. The Russian oligarchs with a significant role in the survival of Putin's regime, mentioned in the previous section, are one example, as individuals with a role in the evolution of international events (and on the subsequent, hopefully temporary, downfall of international law). The other side of the barricade, of course, has its own tycoons—see Bezos, Musk, Mittal, Gates, Zuckerberg etc.—equally entangled with global affairs. After all, international law has always been intimately connected to property: born from the desire of European monarchs to plunder unhindered during colonisation, it later grew fed by the capitalist need for markets and resources, and was matured in the 20th century with an international rule of law meant to satisfy the international finance institutions (Al Attar 2021). What seems to be different now is that the indecently rich have a correspondent in politics, even in democracies: the indecently powerful. Speaking in Johannesburg in 2018 on the occasion of the celebration of Nelson Mandela's centenary, former US president Barak Obama referred to what he declared to be a universal diminution/loss of credibility in the international system and the emergence of what he called "strongman politics":

> And a politics of fear and resentment and retrenchment began to appear, and that kind of politics is now on the move. It's on the move at a pace that would have seemed unimaginable just a few years ago. . . . Strongman politics are ascendant suddenly, whereby elections and some pretense of democracy are maintained—the form of it—but those in power seek to undermine every institution or norm that gives democracy meaning.
>
> In the West, you've got far-right parties that oftentimes are based not just on platforms of protectionism and closed borders, but also on barely hidden racial nationalism. Many developing countries now are looking at China's model of authoritarian control combined with mercantilist capitalism as preferable to the messiness of democracy. Who needs free speech as long as the economy is going good? The free press is under attack. Censorship and state control of media is on the rise. Social media—once seen as a mechanism to promote knowledge and understanding and solidarity—has proved to be just as effective promoting hatred and paranoia and propaganda and conspiracy theories.
>
> (Obama 2018)

Although Obama does not mention any names, it is not too difficult to guess at least some of the strong-arm state actors to which he was referring. His address is worth careful consideration, not only for the message it contains, but also for suggesting the emergence of another class of non-state actors that does not yet appear to have received scrutiny in discussion forums. There exists a class of non-state actors that carries out the strongman's strong-arm political actions, the consequences of which may result in the outcomes that Obama refers to earlier. These actors/operatives may be international or domestic but are more likely to be transnational. They may be prominent, deliberately so, as a demonstration of power—to which the army of January 6 rioters which occupied the US Congress could be said to belong. Other operatives may be lone wolves or small groups whose anonymity and invisibility are vital for success and survival—perhaps in the general locale of Russian oligarchs who meet unfortunate fatal accidents. Indeed, state actors, particularly those whose position and authority rest upon principles of law and democracy, rights and freedoms (generally) cannot afford to be directly linked with those forces carrying out the application of their strongman politics.

However, in the current era of population growth and increasing demand for fundamental essentials of food, water, and shelter, of climate change and demands for clean energy and the essential materials and resources to provide it, the international era of "strongman politics" and international conflict threatened and actual, some conventional entrenched views on the theory and nature of international law warrant re-examination. Are strongmen of the ilk of President Putin becoming non-state actors in view of their actions' radical departure from the rule of law and the will of the huge majority of the population? African strongmen (dictators) have been deemed so, which is why they were tried as individuals before the International Criminal Court, rather than having their actions attributed to their country. But for a democratic country, this perspective is troubling.

But one does not need to be a plutocrat to play a role (to be more than a spectator, that is) relevant to international law. Julian Assange has been pursued by US authorities in a lengthy campaign that has continued for a number of years to have his extradition finalised in order to face sedition charges over his leaking of thousands of US government documents through WikiLeaks, which led to CIA Director Pompeo labelling him "a non-state hostile intelligence service often abetted by state actors" (Endrem 2017). Obviously, an overenthusiastic description of a high-profile individual as a non-state actor primarily on the basis of that profile can degenerate into the legal perspective being overtaken and forgotten—and more generally, creates the danger of the whole discussion on non-state actors descending into the theatre of the absurd. Still, two points should be retained from this subsection as relevant to the overall argument of the book: first, that official function (or lack thereof) is not the end of the story when examining the role of a putative non-state actor and second, that even for an entity the role of which has been examined for many decades, namely, the individual, the discussion remains open.

The Covid-19 Pandemic and Non-State Actors

International law has its strongwomen as well. In 2020, when flexing her muscles and declaring that she "will go hard and go early" with severely restrictive measures meant to combat the Covid-19 pandemic, New Zealand Prime Minister Jacinda Ardern was putting herself above the international law norms requiring that any restriction of rights comes after a careful balancing of the options, and respects the conditions of legality, necessity, and proportionality. Prime Minister Ardern was not alone in this attitude but only overly enthusiastic. Aside from a handful of countries who took a more moderate approach, leaders all over the world turned overnight into strongmen/strongwomen and rushed to send their countries into long and severe lockdowns, with devastating impacts on human rights (see, for example, Ferstman and Fagan 2020; Bennoune 2020; Radavoi and Quirico 2022). What the states ignored when dealing with the pandemic was the simple truth that "[a]ny meaningful human rights law approach to COVID-19 must be holistic and recognize the breadth of the challenges to both economic, social, and cultural rights, and civil and political rights. It must be grounded in the threat posed by the disease but also address responses to it and implicate a wide range of state and nonstate actors" (Bennoune 2020, 166; emphasis added).

Indeed, the non-state actor did not play the healthy role that it could, and should, have in ensuring the balance required by international human rights law between legitimate anti-pandemic measures and equally legitimate rights such as the rights to freedom of movement, of expression, to data privacy, or to work, during the 2 years or so of pandemic. Instead, non-state actors contributed to the hysteria, either by legitimising the unilateral approach of 'going hard and early' (mass media), or by tacitly condoning harsh, imbalanced governmental restrictions like banning the unvaccinated from the workplace (trade unions, the business environment). Some non-state actors tried to speak out but were simply ignored by the state (for example, international NGOs like Amnesty International, or IGOs such as the World Health Organisation repeatedly but in vain reminding governments about the necessity and proportionality requirement). The individual, perhaps succumbing to the climate of fear perpetuated by the state and the mass media, was complacent and docile, seemingly in disagreement with the statement of Fionnuala Ní Aoláin, UN special rapporteur on counterterrorism and human rights, that "a life in which your physical health is guaranteed but every other right has been taken away is meaningless" (cited in Bruney 2020). The explanation, according to Aoláin, is fear: "When people are afraid for their own health and that of their family members, we tend not to balance that immediate fear with the long-term harm to our freedoms and rights."

A deeper exploration of the causes behind the greying out of the non-state actors in times of pandemics is beyond the scope of this book. This subsection's aim is only to point out that there are circumstances where the non-state actor—including the rural community, if the case as argued in the next chapter is accepted as valid—forgets about its role and becomes a docile spectator to the monologue of the one actor monopolising the scene—the state.

The Fourth Industrial Revolution and Non-State Actors

In 2016, Klaus Schwab, founder and chairman of the World Economic Forum, published his groundbreaking and controversial book *The Fourth Industrial Revolution* under the auspices of the forum. Much of the work was based on ongoing projects and initiatives developed, discussed, and challenged at recent forum gatherings and continues to be an ongoing theme of the forum's programme. Schwab (2016) argues that this fourth industrial revolution, which has been in progress at least since the beginning of the current century, fundamentally changes the way that members of society live, work, and relate to each other. It differs from previous revolutions on three fundamental grounds:

- Because of our multifaceted deeply interconnected world, it is evolving at an exponential rather than linear pace, with new technology creating newer and ever more capable technology.
- The combining of multiple technologies leads to unprecedented paradigm shifts in the economy and society, changing not only the "what" and the "how" of doing things but also "who" we are.
- It involves the transformation of entire systems, across and within countries, companies, industries, and society as a whole.

Being built on the digital revolution, the fourth industrial revolution is characterised by a much more ubiquitous and mobile internet, by smaller and more powerful sensors that have become cheaper, and by artificial intelligence (AI) and machine learning. It encompasses the confluence of emerging technology breakthroughs, covering wide-ranging fields such as AI, robotics, the internet of things, autonomous vehicles, three-dimensional printing, nanotechnology, biotechnology, materials science, energy storage, and quantum computing, to name a few. Many of these innovations are in their infancy.

Schwab acknowledges that the scale and breadth of this unfolding technological revolution will usher in economic, social, and cultural changes of phenomenal proportion impacting state actors, society, and individuals. The global nature of the global connectivity on both institutional and personal bases will inevitably result in a transfer of the power equilibriums from established state actors to emerging state actors. It will also bring transfers from state actors to non-state actors and from established, identifiable institutions to diffuse networks with flexible structures. This scenario is one to which state actors must be prepared to adapt, by being willing, prepared, and proactive in interacting with non-state actors to manage and maintain as much control as possible over that power equilibrium transfer.

Accordingly, while Schwab can wax lyrical about the potential positive outcomes for economies, society, and the individual, he also warns of a darker negative of the revolution. The power equilibrium shift in favour of non-state actors can also change the character of the national and international security equilibrium. The technological development that brings benefits also brings potential for the development of a new generation of powerful, autonomous, mobile, and cheap weaponry that will be more easily accessible to armed insurgent and terrorist non-state actors. Commentaries focussing on the security and military perspective of the revolution's technological development argue that these technologies are shifting the military balance between states and non-state actors in favour of the latter, and express alarm that the revolution will provide insurgent and terrorist groups with capabilities that, until very recently, were the preserve of large, powerful, wealthy states (e.g., Hammes 2019).

Other impacts regarding non-state actors may be an unprecedented increase in the power of the corporation, as warned by one of the interviewees in a major study on the future of humanity, undertaken in 2018 by the Pew Research Center:

> Without explicit efforts to humanize AI design, we'll see a population that is needed for purchasing, but not creating. This population will need to be controlled and AI will provide the means for this control: law enforcement by drones, opinion manipulation by bots, cultural homogeny through synchronized messaging, election systems optimized from big data, and a geopolitical system dominated by corporations that have benefited from increasing efficiency and lower operating costs.
> (Anderson, Rainie, and Luchsinger 2018, 61)

More generally, most of the Pew Research Center's interviewees, regardless of whether they were optimistic or not concerning the general impacts of AI on society, expressed "concerns about the long-term impact of these new tools on the essential elements of being human" (Anderson, Rainie, and Luchsinger 2018, 2). These concerns are especially valid if one believes the growing body of scientists, philosophers, and futurists (see generally Shanahan 2015) who warn that in the not-too-distant future, robots endowed with AI and with instantaneous access to the corpus of knowledge that is the internet as well as the 'internet of things', as the apotheosis of the fourth revolution's interconnectivity, will develop their own decision-making capacity and independent action (the so-called Singularity Hypothesis). This then raises a number of fundamental questions in a legal context—for example, does such a robot acquire rights and responsibilities? Does it acquire legal personality? And does it warrant recognition as a representative of a new generation of non-state actors? For example, would it meet Worster's fundamental characteristic of function or Art's fundamental driver of power? The limitations are now more legal, regulatory, and ethical than technical.

The commentary in this chapter hopefully adds meaningful material to the mountain of debate and ongoing differences of opinion as to what is a non-state actor. As a conclusion to this chapter, it is posited that even if comfortable, widely adoptable criteria could be generally agreed upon, it would probably still not answer the fundamental questions for very long, such is the rapidly changing state of regional and international events. By way of demonstration as to how far the debate has already moved on, Morss's (1991) proposed description of a non-state actor seems rather inadequate today. Morss (1991) refers to the considerable size, transnational constituency, formal recognition by governments and IGOs, and international political impact in order to decide whether an entity is a relevant global player or not. The first two qualifications can be shown to be fully outdated in light of the considerations relating to the emergence of the fourth industrial revolution, and to civil society's contribution in many different ways to the survival of Ukraine during the current Russian invasion. The third and fourth qualifications may still have some validity, but not to the extent originally envisaged. As evidenced by civil society's readiness for public protest, even if confrontational to the sovereign authority (see protests in China against the Party's zero-Covid policy resulting in a relaxation of that policy), state actor approval for non-state actor access to political arenas is no longer compulsory.

With these in mind, this contribution now turns to examining the rural community's candidature to non-state actor status.

References

Ainsworth, David. 2023. "Who's Sending Aid to Ukraine?" *Devex*. www.devex.com/news/funding-tracker-who-s-sending-aid-to-ukraine-102887.

Al Attar, Mohsen. 2021. "Follow the Money: The Misery of International Law." *Opinio Juris*, February 25.

Alston, Philippe. 2005b. "The 'Not-a-Cat' Syndrome: Can the International Human Rights Regime Accommodate Non-State Actors?" In *Non-State Actors and Human Rights*, edited by Philippe Alston, 3–36. Oxford: Oxford University Press.

Anderson, Janna, Lee Rainie, and Alex Luchsinger. 2018. *Artificial Intelligence and the Future of Humans*. Washington, DC: Pew Research Center.

Arts, Bas. 2003. "Non-State Actors in Global Governance: Three Faces of Power." Preprints aus der Max-Planck-Projektgruppe Recht der Gemeinschaftsgüter No. 4. Bonn, Germany.

Bennoune, Karima. 2020. "'Lest We Should Sleep': COVID-19 and Human Rights." *American Journal of International Law* 114 (4): 666–76.

Bruney, Gabrielle. 2020. "My Concern Is That Authoritarians May Use COVID as a Cover." *Esquire*, June 15.

Chan, Isaac. 2022. "The Latest in a Long Line: Ukraine's International Legion and a History of Foreign Fighters." *Harvard International Review*, September 2, 2022. https://hir.harvard.edu/the-latest-in-a-long-line-ukraines-international-legion-and-a-history-of-foreign-fighters/.

Côté, Charles-Emmanuel. 2020. "Introduction: Non-State Actors, Changing Actors and Subjects of International Law." In *Changing Actors in International Law*, edited by Karen N. Scott, Kathleen Claussen, Charles-Emmanuel Côté, and Atsuko Kanehara, 1–24. Leiden: Brill.

Endrem, Robert. 2017. "CIA Director Pompeo Calls WikiLeaks a 'Hostile Intelligence Service'." *NBC News*, April 14.

Ferstman, Carla, and Andrew Fagan, eds. 2020. *Covid-19, Law and Human Rights: Essex Dialogues*. University of Essex. www.essex.ac.uk/research-projects/covid-19-law-and- human-rights-essex-dialogues.

Hammes, T. X. 2019. "Technology Converges; Non-State Actors Benefit." Governance in an Emerging World, Hoover Institution, Harvard University, February 25.

International Law Association (ILA). 2010. "Non-State Actors." Report, The Hague Conference.

———. 2016. "Final Report on Non-State Actors." Johannesburg Conference.

Li, Yan. 2022. "Non-State Actors, New Disruptors." *China-US Focus*, April 27.

Morss, Elliott R. 1991. "The New Global Players: How They Compete and Collaborate." *World Development* 19 (1): 55–64.

Nasiritousi, Naghmeh, Mattias Hjerpe, and Karin Bäckstrand. 2016. "Normative Arguments for Non-State Actor Participation in International Policymaking Processes: Functionalism, Neocorporatism or Democratic Pluralism?" *European Journal of International Relations* 22 (4): 920–43.

Obama, Barak. 2018. "Sixteenth Nelson Mandela Annual Lecture." *Nelson Mandela Foundation*, July 17, 2018. www.nelsonmandela.org/content/page/annual-lecture-2018.

Pearlman, Wendy, and Kathleen Cunningham. 2012. "Nonstate Actors, Fragmentation, and Conflict Processes." *Journal of Conflict Resolution* 56 (1): 3–15.

Perera, Suda. 2015. "Political Engagement with Non-State Actors in Areas of Limited Statehood." Developmental Leadership Program, State of the Art Series No. 5, University of Birmingham. www.dlprog.org.

Radavoi, Ciprian N., and Ottavio Quirico. 2022. "Socioeconomic Rights in the Age of Pandemics: Covid-19 Large-Scale Lockdowns Have Exposed the Weakness of the Right to Work." *Journal of Human Rights* 21 (1): 73–90.

Rosenblat, Mariana Plaizola. 2022. "The Role of Transnational Civil Society in Shaping International Values, Policies, and Law." *Chicago Journal of International Law* 23 (1): 144–60.

Schmidt, Blake, and Scott Carpenter. 2022. "Who Are Russia's Oligarchs and Can They Sway Putin?" *Bloomberg*, March 21.

Schwab, Klaus. 2016. *The Fourth Industrial Revolution*. New York: Crown Business.

Shanahan, Murray. 2015. *The Technological Singularity*. Cambridge, MA: MIT Press.

Vavra, Shannon. 2023. "Ukraine Intelligence Busts Spies Helping Russia Hit Energy Supplies." *Daily Beast*, January 20.

Worster, William T. 2016. "Relative International Legal Personality of Non-State Actors." *Brooklyn Journal of International Law* 42 (1): 207–73.

Ziener, Markus, and Laura King. 2022. "In Ukraine War, a Shadowy Key Player Emerges Russia's Private Army." *Los Angeles Times*, October 5.

2 Rural Communities
Non-State Actors?

The View From Positivism: Rural Communities in International Law Regimes

The classical international legal positivism that emerged in the 19th century grounded the power of law in the fact that it is "made by man and, by extension, human collectivities called states" (Onuf 1982, 2). Stemming from state centrism in the international order, positivism assumed that international law has its origin in the will and consensus of states, the only rule-makers, who act via signing treaties and creating customary law. The reality that states (and international governmental organisations) remain the exclusive international law-makers has not changed with the rise of the non-state actors' role: "[t]he upstream influence wielded by some non-state actors can help ignite new law-making initiatives or orientate ongoing law-making undertakings but this is insufficient to elevate these actors to the status of law-makers" (D'Aspremont 2011, 25). The International Law Association (ILA) similarly found little support for the assertion that non-state actors can be international law-makers, except for the capacity of armed groups to make unilateral legal commitments, binding (if at all) only on themselves (ILA 2016, 25–26).

Classical positivism as a scholarly approach to international law has been under attack over the last century by various schools of thought (realism, and various forms of revived naturalism, for example), and its retreat led to the creation of several modern variants of international legal positivism. As a result, positivism in international law is now an ambiguous term, with various adaptions needed to save it in the current era of pluralisation and increased concern with humanitarian action. However, a more restrictive conception of positivism, limited to the use of formal standards to ascertain what the law is on a certain topic, has survived given its utility as a tool to understand the growing complexity of the world. Proponents called this conception 'reductionism' (D'Aspremont 2012). However, it has also been referred to as 'thematic' positivism: one restricted to "the analysis of positive law, without offering any critique, without reflecting on its basis, without measuring it against the exigencies of justice" (Kolb 2016, 103).

DOI: 10.4324/9781003385318-3

In this limited understanding, international legal positivism accepts a role for non-state actors, not as law-makers, but as participants specifically listed in several international law regimes, where they are endowed by states with rights and duties. Relying on a view of positivism restricted to the use of formal standards for identifying the rules of international law, a leading scholar involved in the investigation of the non-state actor's status and role in the international law, Professor Jean d'Aspremont, notes that formal law ascertainment embeds a certain degree of indeterminacy (D'Aspremont 2011, 24). Among the strategies devised by positivists to overcome the non-self-sufficiency of formal standards of law ascertainment is the social thesis, which supplements the textual analysis of sources of international law with understandings derived from the practice of law-applying authorities, among which are non-state actors. This leads d'Aspremont to conclude that "non-state actors are very instrumental in the communitarian semantics necessary to give meaning to law-ascertainment criteria" and hence, "these actors may well occasionally have a formal international legal personality derived from their rights and duties" (D'Aspremont 2011, 25). Their international legal personality is formal in the sense that it is explicitly acknowledged in the state-centric lawmaking process (positivism) and is occasional in the sense that it surfaces in specific regimes only: armed groups in international humanitarian law, multinational enterprises (MNEs) in international environmental law and international human rights law, and so on. The question remains whether rural communities are among the non-state entities whose social practice can serve for international law ascertainment. If they are, then, in the words of the ILA definition of non-state actors, rural communities "perform functions . . . with real and potential effects on international law" (ILA 2016, 4) and thus qualify as non-state actors.

Communities in general have been identified as playing, under a number of international law instruments, roles in the adoption of decisions or measures, the carrying out of activities, the sharing of benefits, the creation of mechanisms and procedures, and even the elaboration of international instruments (Urbinati 2015, 128). Rural communities are usually not specifically mentioned as such but can be indirectly identified as endowed with rights and obligations in several international instruments: treaties, instruments for their application (guidelines), and soft law (declarations, recommendations) emerging from states as the only subjects of international law. Instruments attached to treaties are relevant because they are themselves tools for reducing the indeterminacy embedded in treaties, whereas soft law, while not binding, counts because it shows its creators' (states) intentions for the future (Urbinati 2015, 124).

The easiest identification of rural communities in international instruments stems from references to occupations such as farmers, pastoralists, and peasants. Although a non-binding instrument, the United Nations (UN) Declaration on the Rights of Peasants and Other People Working in Rural Areas (commonly known as the Peasants Declaration) is important as "the culmination of a long-term struggle that peasant movements directly led from grassroots to global level, developing a novel approach to agency and representation in international policymaking" (Cotula 2022, 91). Defining peasants as people who engage in small-scale agricultural production, who rely significantly on non-monetised ways of organising labour, and who have a special attachment to the land (Article 1.1.), the Peasants Declaration recognises new rights (to land, seeds, and biodiversity) in international law. This a significant development given that, until recently, the concept of land rights in the international human rights framework was developed primarily in relation to indigenous rights.

The concept of peasants' rights builds on previous developments in 'soft' non-binding international law, such as Agenda 21, which spoke of farmers' rights. Defining them as "all rural people who derive their livelihood from activities such as farming, fishing and forest harvesting," Agenda 21 notes in paragraph 32 that "farmers must conserve their physical environment as they depend on it for their sustenance" and calls for the government to involve them in the drafting of all sustainability-relevant policies. As for binding international instruments relevant to the rights of peasants, farmers, and people living and working in rural areas, the UN Convention to Combat Desertification in Those Countries Experiencing Serious Drought and/or Desertification (Desertification Convention), for example, stipulates in Article 10.2(f) that national action programmes should provide for effective participation of local communities, "particularly resource users, including farmers and pastoralists and their representative organizations, in policy planning, decision-making, and implementation and review of national action programmes." Similarly, the International Treaty on Plant Genetic Resources for Food and Agriculture (Plant Treaty) provides in Article 9.2 that the contracting parties will protect farmers' rights, including the recognition of the "right to participate in making decisions, at the national level, on matters related to the conservation and sustainable use of plant genetic resources for food and agriculture."

Some regional instruments refer not to farmers individually, but to their organisations. The Partnership Agreement between the European Union and the African, Caribbean, and Pacific countries (Cotonou Agreement), signed in 2000 to support the sustainable economic, cultural, and social development of the partner countries, lists in Article 6 the non-state actors relevant to the agreement as being the private sector, economic and social partners including trade unions organisations, and civil society in all its forms according to national characteristics. The first Joint Declaration attached to the agreement acknowledges that the latter may include "human rights groups and agencies, grassroots organisations, women's associations, youth organisations, child-protection organisations, environmental movements, farmers' organisations, consumers' associations, religious organisations, development support structures (NGOs [non-governmental organisations], teaching and research establishments), cultural associations and the media."

Sometimes rural communities feature in international instruments under the broader umbrella of local communities. Instruments relevant to the natural environment assign rights to rural communities referring to them broadly as 'local communities'; however, the rural character is easily inferable from the subject matter of the instrument and the wording of the text. This is, for instance, the case of the Convention on Biological Diversity (Biodiversity Convention), which lays down in Article 8(j) that states should "respect, preserve and maintain knowledge, innovations and practices of indigenous and local communities embodying traditional lifestyles relevant for the conservation and sustainable use of biological diversity." Guidelines to the Ramsar Convention, the Convention on Wetlands of International Importance Especially as Waterfowl Habitat (Convention on Wetlands) also sets out the framework for participatory management by local and indigenous communities, while the convention itself is very much about rural livelihoods.

Instruments focussed on the cultural rather than the natural environment also empower rural communities. In this case, the rural character of the community is deducible from the circumstances. The Convention Concerning the Protection of the World Cultural and Natural Heritage (World Heritage Convention) uses the word 'community' scarcely, which was explained in the literature by the fact that in the case of tangible heritage, protection is often needed against, rather than for, the local community: "[w]hile past communities are often the creators of what is significant in the sites and are believed to establish the 'outstanding universal value' required for an inscription on the World Heritage List, present-day local populations often come in only as a disturbing factor, as those who build the high-rises and bridges in old towns or who log, poach or illegally cultivate in the nature reserves" (Brumann 2015, 277). The communities referred to are rural, given the location of the endangered outstanding universal value heritage, but also given the activities listed in this quote as a source of danger. This reading of the Heritage Convention scope provides an interesting additional angle to the rural community as a non-state actor: the rural community as a villain against which the international law protection is needed. On the other hand, the positive role of the local (rural) communities has more recently been emphasised in the context of the tangible heritage during the 40th anniversary of the Convention in 2012, being celebrated under the overall theme, "World Heritage and Sustainable Development: The Role of Local Communities."

Much more often is the community mentioned in the context of intangible heritage, where the Convention for the Safeguarding of the Intangible Cultural Heritage adopted in 2003 provides in Article 15 for the "participation of communities that create, maintain and transmit such heritage" and for these communities being actively involved in intangible heritage management. Importantly, local communities can even become involved in the elaboration of international instruments for the protection of traditional knowledge,

Rural Communities 27

traditional cultural expressions, folklore, and genetic resources under the auspices of the World Intellectual Property Organization.

The international law on international watercourses is also highly relevant to rural communities. For example, the Nile River system collectively flows through Tanzania, Uganda, Kenya, Burundi, Rwanda, the Democratic Republic of the Congo, Sudan, Ethiopia, South Sudan, and Egypt—and the livelihood of many rural communities along its course entirely depends on it. The river has been the subject of a series of long-standing treaties commencing in 1885 on its water usage but is still the source of controversy over plans by states in the upper reaches to build dams for their own development, which adversely affects states downstream, whose own economic development and rural communities along the course of the river may be drastically impacted.

Finally, several important international instruments on indigenous peoples necessarily apply to rural indigenous communities. First, even though in most developed countries a significant proportion of the indigenous population now resides in cities, this proportion is still far less than the proportion of non-indigenous peoples living in urban settlements: in Australia, for instance, the most recent available data from the Australian Bureau of Statistics show that the latter is approximately double (72.6% as compared to 37.4%). Second, the rights protected often have a rural component. Indigenous self-determination, a fundamental principle behind major international instruments, is now accepted by democratic countries; legislative frameworks have been established to give indigenous populations the right to use their land for traditional purposes, to participate in decision-making about future land use, and to negotiate the economic and social benefits of resource extraction on their territory. The UN Declaration on the Rights of Indigenous Peoples, for example, establishes in Article 30 that military activities cannot take place in the lands of indigenous peoples unless justified by a public interest or otherwise freely agreed with them. Article 32 of the same instrument lays down the right of the indigenous communities to veto an economic project affecting their lands. Similarly, Article 16(2) of the International Labour Organization Indigenous and Tribal Peoples Convention, adopted in 1989, states that relocation of indigenous peoples in cases of large-scale industrial projects cannot be given effect without their prior informed consent. Both military activities and large-scale development projects can only be conceived in non-urban spaces; therefore, these provisions, which empower a rural community to resist their own government, are relevant from the positivist angle for understanding the role of rural communities as non-state actors.

The View From New Haven: Mobilised Rural Communities in International Law

The New Haven School rejected "an innocent-appearing insistence that the prime and unique task of legal scholarship is simply to ascertain what the law is" (McDougal 1953, 144). Unlike the positivists, scholars in the New Haven tradition do not focus on 'legal norms' but propose a comprehensive analysis of all the variables that affect decision-making (Reisman 1992, 119–20). Accordingly, while positivism views the law from the perspective of the receiver of commands, who is tasked with interpreting the command laid down in authoritative texts and the procedures for obedience to them, the New Haven School of jurisprudence adopts the perspective of the decision-maker, whose main task is to make the appropriate choices for the relevant community (Reisman 1992, 119).

'Decision-maker' in this perspective goes beyond the state with its courts, governments, or parliaments, because "international law is most realistically observed . . . as the whole process of authoritative decision in which patterns of authority and patterns of control are appropriately conjoined" (Suzuki 1974, 30). Seeing law as patterns of authority and control, the New Haven School blends law into power, speaking not of rules but of policies. Indeed, in the words of the school's creators, "[n]one who deal with law, however defined, can escape policy when policy is defined as the making of important decisions which affect the distribution of values" (Lasswell and McDougal 1943, 207).

By conjoining law with power, the school is evocative of the political realism proposed by Hans Morgenthau. Similarities between the two approaches to international law, noted in academia (Hathaway 2007, 555), include a critical approach to positivism and the attention paid to state power as essential to understanding state behaviour. There are, however, fundamental differences. First, the New Haven School sees the state as the main holder of power but not the only one: the state may hold the formal power, but other entities exercise actual authority, to various degrees, as well (Waters 2007, 456). Even the individual "can now participate, whether directly or through the mediation of groups, in the processes of decision that affect their lives" (Reisman, Wiessner, and Willard 2007, 576–77). Second, power is not the only value that actors in the international system attempt to maximise, but also values such as wealth, enlightenment, skill, respect, and generally everything circumscribed by the concept of human dignity (McDougal 1960, 349).

In sum, New Haven scholars look at the interstices of power to see how a variety of actors compete to have their values and interests prevail, and to unveil the complex social processes that shape law in practice. In this sense, the New Haven School steps in the footprints of American legal realism, well summed up in the famous statement of Oliver Wendell Holmes: "The prophecies of what the courts will do in fact, and nothing more pretentious, are what I mean by the law" (Holmes 1897, 462). The New Haven School deals with the international law by scrutinising, with methods borrowed from social sciences, the prophecies of what decision-makers in the international plane—states mainly, but not only—will do in fact, and why. Accordingly, the New Haven School has been referred to as 'sociolegal realism' (Levit 2007, 419).

Importantly, an essential addition to the predictive and descriptive dimensions of the New Haven approach is the normative one: how to ensure the right decision in the circumstances (Falk 1995). The normative character has led some scholars to underline the similitudes between the New Haven School and the natural law tradition (e.g., Reisman 1992, 119), a rapprochement that makes the former dangerously biased and "[opens] the way for partisan or subjective policies disguised as law" (Schachter 1985, 267). Despite this criticism, the New Haven approach has passed the test of time, as its conceptual technique for mapping the relevant decision-making processes—briefly summarised later—fits well the pluralism of the globalised world (Koh 2007).

Authoritative and controlling decision in the international plane—which to New Haven scholars *is* international law—emerges from three interrelated phases: social interaction (where people and groups interact to maximise their preferences) is followed by a process of claims (directed towards decision-makers) and then by a process of authoritative decision (Suzuki 1974, 33). In order to fully and realistically capture this process, a functional approach using a set of relevant variables is employed: *participants* in social interaction, their *perspectives* (their value demands), the *situations* involved (the social conditions under which interactions take place), *bases of power* (resources on which each participant draws), *strategies* (how participants make use of their resources), and *outcomes* and *effects* (the immediate and the long-term results of the process, respectively) (Suzuki 1974, 23–30). This mapping procedure is "designed to minimize the chances of overlooking pertinent factors and relationships [and] enables the lawyer and policy-scientist to operate with a realistic sense of the relevant processes" (Reisman, Wiessner, and Willard 2007, 579). In understanding this process, the lawyer and the policy scientist must bear in mind that 'decision-makers' are, albeit to varying degrees, all the participants in the social process described earlier (interaction—claims—decision), because the two components of power—authority (related to shared values as indication of appropriate behaviour) and control (related to resources employed to influence others' behaviour)—are to some extent found even in entities apparently devoid of any power.

One example of rural communities involved, as participants, in an international process of authoritative and controlling decision are those mobilised against foreign investment projects. A common case is that of rural communities opposing landfills, and generally the dumping of garbage in their vicinity. In *Vito G. Gallo v. Government of Canada* (2011), for example, mass local protests by First Nations communities blocked the dumping of garbage on their lands, which led to international litigation between the American investor, Mr. Gallo, and Canada in the form of a claim of expropriation before the Permanent Court of Arbitration. The investment had come soon after a highly controversial decision of Toronto City Council allowed shipping of more than 20 million tonnes of garbage to the abandoned Adams Mine, almost 400 kilometres to the north, in the lands of the First Nations. Prior to and after the decision, inhabitants of the affected rural areas had shown their opposition in various ways, from rallies to railroad blockades. It is under these circumstances that in 2002, the investor purchased the Adams Mine, which already had certain administrative approvals required for its use as a waste disposal site. However, in 2004, the Ontario legislature enacted the *Adams Mine Lake Act* prohibiting the disposal of waste at the Adams Mine. The tribunal found that the investing company was in fact Canadian, since the alleged American investor, Mr. Gallo, at the time of enactment of the act, was not yet the owner of the enterprise. As this was a case of international investment law, the tribunal declined jurisdiction, ordering the claimant to pay the costs ($450,000) of Canada as well.

Other cases where rural communities stood against international investment are in mining. In *Bear Creek Mining Corp. v. Republic of Peru* (2017), the International Centre for Settlement of Investment Disputes (ICSID) found in favour of a Canadian investor who had their investment in oil and gas exploitation obstructed by protests from neighbouring rural communities. *Lupaka Gold Corp. v. Republic of Peru*, ongoing at ICSID at the time of this writing, concerns a gold mine, also in Peru with a Canadian investor, similarly halted by community protests. The claimant built its argument on the claim that Peru failed to provide assistance when the mining project was hindered by local mobilisation. All these cases fit neatly within the analytical framework designed by the New Haven School to explain international law as authoritative and controlling the decision. The three steps are clearly delineated: (a) social interaction when the community gets mobilised against the investment project; (b) claims presented when the community has reached a certain level of mobilisation and a coherent position regarding the investment; and (c) claims assessed and decisions made by the final decision-maker: the investor if they decide to halt the project and not take further action, the state if it manages to arbitrate between the investor and the community, or international arbitral tribunals if the investor has the legal base (such as a bilateral investment treaty between their country of incorporation and the host country of the investment) and decides to submit a claim.

The mapping process proposed by the New Haven School indicates the rural community as one *participant* in the decision-making process alongside the investor, civil society, mass media, governmental agencies and other institutions and individuals (lawyers, consultants) specialised in the transnational wealth process, and the international investment arbitral tribunals, such as the ICSID. The *perspectives* of each of these are different—some participants are animated by environmental values, others by the imperative of maintaining social order, and others by the pursuit of wealth. The *situations* in which they interact are also diverse, from physical confrontations and street blockades to negotiations, coercion from police, and, in the end, international investment arbitration between the allegedly expropriated investor and the host state (where the rural community is not a party, but without its actions there would have been no arbitral case in the first place). Participants' *bases of power* vary from mobilisation and numbers in the case of the community, and access to financial and political resources in the case of investors. Their *strategies* reflect their asymmetric power: communities are often trying to build networks and to enlist the support of the media, while investors pull strings in the government or openly threaten the host state with international investment arbitration, possibly leading to hundreds of millions of dollars in compensation for the alleged expropriation.

Unfortunately for the rural communities involved, the outcomes are often in favour of the investor, who sometimes makes more profit from the arbitral award than they would have made from the halted business (Alvik 2020). Occasionally, however, the community manages to build on its authoritative (value-related) power and even accumulate a certain degree of control (coercion-related) power to obtain a favourable outcome, as occurred in *Gallo*.

International investment law is a mix of public and private international law, featuring the investor's treaty-based right to bring claims against the host state through procedures that are governed by private arrangements. Rural communities can influence decision-making in this framework, as shown earlier, but are not a party to the dispute. They can, however, become a party to disputes in "pure" private international law, when class action by villagers affected by foreign corporations—usually via local subsidiaries—is pursued in the courts of the corporation's home country. Until recently, this was made very difficult by the strict application of the doctrine of *forum non conveniens*, but in the last decade changes can be observed, especially when the alleged wrongdoing concerns pollution of the community's air and waters by industrial projects, most often mining. The courts handling *Chandler v. Cape plc* (2012) in England and *Choc v. Hudbay Minerals* (2013) in Canada both applied a theory of direct liability to hold that parent mining companies can owe a legal duty of care directly to persons injured by the actions of their foreign subsidiaries when they exercise a high degree of control over said subsidiaries. In *Lungowe v Vedanta Resources PLC* (2017), the UK Court of Appeals allowed Zambian villagers to sue a parent company in the United Kingdom for water pollution by its Zambian subsidiary, holding that the facts could possibly give rise to a duty of care owed by the parent company directly to the villagers. The case was settled out of court in 2021, as has happened with similar cases, because multinational corporations seek to avoid the reputational loss of a long and highly publicised trial. In another example, following the failure of the tailings dam for the Ok Tedi copper mine in Papua New Guinea, mining giant BHP paid US$86 million to affected villagers in an out-of-court settlement reached in 1996. These examples show how a mobilised rural community can—with or without a trial in a court of law—become a participant and influence decision-making in international discourse.

The View From Constitutionalism: Rural Communities' Moral Standing

The previous two sections focussed on ontological realities: first, the reality that states as sole creators of international law occasionally ascribe roles to rural communities in the application of international law, and second, the reality that states as arbitrators sometimes recognise the values and interests pursued by rural communities as legitimate in international policymaking.

International constitutionalism, the approach proposed in this section, advocates for the application of constitutionalist principles to improve effectiveness, justice, and fairness in international law—similar to the role of constitutionalist principles in domestic jurisdictions (e.g., Peters 2009; Kleinlein 2012; Klabbers 2019). Just as domestic constitutions are built on the common values of a certain group, international constitutionalism is inspired by basic values shared by humanity. As such, international constitutionalism is a natural extension of domestic constitutionalism. It extracts common principles from domestic constitutionalism, while also imposing universal principles. The corollary of this binary relationship is that the state becomes an instrument for the international community to implement its core legal values—those now enshrined in international human rights law (Tomuschat 1999). While positivism sees international law as based on the consent of states, and sociolegal realism sees it as based on policies emerging from competing interests and values, constitutionalism is an epitome of naturalism—which claims that international law is, or should be, built on what is right (Tomuschat 1999, 60–61).

As with the two approaches discussed previously, international constitutionalism is an ontological reality of international law to some extent. Institutionally, the UN is deemed by the most enthusiastic constitutionalist scholars as embedding global constitutionalist aspirations, with the UN Charter being a *de facto* constitution of the international order, since it is superior to any other treaty in the same manner in which domestic constitutions are superior to any other domestic law (Fassbender 1998). Other empirically observable markers of constitutionalism are the limitations to state sovereignty meant to accommodate the protection of human rights, the increasing use of majoritarian decision-making as opposed to state consent, and the legalisation of international dispute settlement, with many courts and tribunals now having quasi-compulsory jurisdiction (Peters 2009). In terms of sources of international law, the best illustration of normativity is the existence of two categories of customary law rules which operate irrespective of the state consenting to them: *jus cogens* norms (customary law rules from which no derogation is permitted) and *erga omnes* obligations (obligations towards the entire international community).

However, in the real world, all these are timid and limited injections of values and principles in the life of international discourse, which is why international constitutionalism when seen as an ontological reality has numerous critics in academia. Some concede that constitutionalism may have had its heydays in the first decade of the new millennium, as an ideological counterbalance to aggressive neoliberal globalisation, but now is in retreat as no longer necessary (Klabbers 2019). Others more bluntly reject it as idealism, noting that the world is in fact highly pluralist, therefore in need of political solutions to conflicting norms, and not of utopian adherence to allegedly universal values (Krisch 2010, 58–68; see Peters 2009, 397 for a comprehensive list of critiques against international constitutionalism). As for the UN Charter fulfilling the role of a world constitution, this is factually untenable—suffice to consider how incapable the UN has been to prevent or punish 'unconstitutional' behaviour such as the groundless invasions of Iraq and Ukraine by the United States and Russia, respectively. Accordingly, some scholars argue that international constitutionalism is more "a frame of mind," "a perspective . . . or at least a vision" (Klabbers, Peters, and Ulfstein 2009). In short, a desideratum rather than an ontological reality.

For the purpose of this book—to show that the rural community has a place under the sun of international law—this lack of a unitary approach to constitutionalism is not an impediment. Positivism is contested as well, as is the contemporary relevance of the New Haven School (and pretty much everything else in the theory of international law). For authors engaged in the application rather than the creation of theory, the solution is either to find a lowest common denominator among conflicting theories or to choose a theory to go with. The first section of this chapter, in discussing positivism, went with the lowest common denominator, delineating positivism as the state consent as 'positivized' in treaties and other instruments, which in turn allows for the participation of rural communities in the international law, in specific areas. The second section in this chapter went with the theory that deems the New Haven School as still relevant to contemporary realities; based on this, the rural community as a participant in social interaction was found to be a non-state actor insofar as it imposes its values and interests, in the competitive process of persuading decision-makers. The third section of this chapter relies on the lowest common denominator of constitutionalist theories to argue that rural communities have the right to participate in international law not because a treaty says so and not because its power, when mobilised against injustice, enables it to do so, but because this is the right thing.

The common denominator of constitutionalist theories is the orientation towards individuals—as members of the global constitutional community—and their needs and rights. As public international law has incrementally turned "from an inter-state order into an order committed to the international community and the individual," it now contains "at least traces of constitutional virtues like human rights, democracy, good governance, separation of powers and judicial control" (Kleinlein 2012, 81–82). But the operationalisation of these virtues is unthinkable in the absence of participation; therefore, "participation of *affected* individuals is a necessary feature of constitutionalisation" (Kleinlein 2011, 41; emphasis added). In other words, "discourse on issues of international law must . . . be couched in language that allows everyone *affected* by its operation to make its voice heard, to fully grasp arguments invoked by others and thus to engage in meaningful dialogue permitting to highlight on a common basis of understanding any controversial issues" (Tomuschat 1999, 28; emphasis added). The instruments discussed in the first section of this chapter enshrined this principle with regard to specific areas of international governance, such as combating desertification or managing biodiversity, but this positivist reading is not enough in a constitutionalist perspective: any affected individual should have a voice, and not only those affected by desertification or those who can contribute to biodiversity management.

Individuals are generally affected by transnational activities as communities defined spatially, hence the need to participate as a group in relevant decision-making. Cities for instance are terrorists' target of choice for obvious reasons: they are an accumulation of people and of major infrastructure that is sometimes crucial for the functioning of the whole state, so an urban attack will ensure the highest publicity nationally and globally. As affected individuals, urban citizens now have—through their elected representatives (mayors, councils)—a voice in international law (Aust and Nijman 2021). Cities are, for example, required to cooperate in the global fight against terrorism by the Counter-Terrorism Committee of the UN Security Council (UNSC Committee Chair 2019). One forum where they cooperate is the *Strong Cities Network*, a coalition of more than 140 cities which according to their website, promotes "city leadership as a key tenet of global [terrorism] prevention efforts, shaping international policy agendas at all levels." This and the fact that cities are now policy and standard setters in other areas of governance concerning almost exclusively the urban referential space (drug trafficking, human trafficking, certain types of pollution etc.) has led one scholar to note that "a sort of lawmaking, even if informal, is underway when cities shape international security discourses, participate in transnational networks and advance global normative solutions" (Rodiles 2021, 224). Additional arguments supporting cities' non-state actor status are the fact that they occasionally pursue policies opposed to their own governments on the international plane, as in the case of immigration sanctuary cities in the United States, and the fact that they can appear in international proceedings at the European Court of Justice.

These are strong arguments, but the rich literature on "cities and international law" seems to downplay a few important aspects. First, some of the problems that cities are called upon to resolve from their new status in international law are global problems created by the cities themselves, such as overpopulation, pollution of all sorts, and generally unsustainable development. For example, when UN Habitat (2018) states that "[m]uch of the 2030

Agenda will be 'fought and won' in urban centres, where more than half the world's population live," the implication, explained in the same public statement of the organisation, is that cities need first to reinvent themselves—the "urban development of yesterday will not suffice." That cities, alone or in transnational networks, attempt to improve their own environmental governance issues is laudable; however, the question from the perspective of international constitutionalism is what legitimises their claim of leadership when nearly half of the global population lives in rural areas and often pays the price for the cities' unsustainable development. The struggle against cities dumping their waste on rural communities' space, often under a "foreign investment" arrangement, as shown in the previous section, is one example; other examples are the effects on fish stocks of city waste being dumped in rivers or the effects on irrigation (water availability and prices) of cities' excessive water usage, such as unregulated municipal and domestic gardens watering and car washing.

Further, just as some transnational governance areas concern cities almost exclusively (terrorism, human trafficking, drug trafficking), others concern rural communities almost exclusively, for instance, land-grabbing by multinational corporations, nuclear waste dumping, and village massacres by insurgent groups. If urban residents have a voice on the international plane in matters concerning them directly, so should rural residents, specifically on rural matters with transnational or international dimensions. That is, if the existence of transnational municipal networks is an argument that cities are non-state actors, then this applies to transnational rural networks as well. Indeed, rural localities have long been networking transnationally. *Via Campesina*, for example, an international movement bringing together millions of peasants, landless workers, indigenous people, migrant farmworkers, small and medium-size farmers, and rural women from around the world, struggles according to their website to ensure direct representation of rural communities in global, regional, and national spaces of governance and negotiations. They also influence global standards, for example, those driving and influencing food security.

Still in the area of international networking, it should be noted that the global 'sister city movement', familiar to most readers, is somewhat of a misnomer, as the movement is not restricted to major cities or urban population centres, but may, and does, involve many local government entities and community participation—including rural and remote. For example, Boring, a town of some 8000 people south east of Portland Oregon, United States, has a sister city relationship with Dull, a small village in rural Perth, and with Kinross, Scotland, population uncertain, as well as with Bland, a town of some 6000 people in southwestern New South Wales, Australia (Gibbs et al. 2015).

Admittedly, these examples do not prove that cities and rural communities have an equally strong claim of non-state actor status, in a strictly ontological approach to international constitutionalism. But international constitutionalism is to a large extent a mindset and a vision, a vision mainly embraced and promoted by international law scholars. In this perspective, it is surprising that cohorts of academics dissect, explain, and generally salute the rise to global power of the city, while virtually none look at the role of the other (almost) half of the global population in international law. In parallel with supporting the case for the city as a non-state actor, which sometimes results in stretching doctrine and concepts to accommodate the rising hero of international law, academics should also support the voice of rural communities in international law. When academics state that they "focus on the specific role [that] cities should play in international lawmaking as legitimate representatives of their citizens" (Besson and Martí 2021, 343), they should also focus on the role that representatives of the rural population should play in their quest for justice. Indeed, the struggle of transnational rural networks seems to be fundamentally for justice, whereas transnational municipal networks fundamentally aim for control, operationalising their power in order to gain decision-maker status in various matters, including some where rural communities should also have a voice.

Taking the Argument Further: Remote Communities in International Law

The invisibility curtain drawn in international law upon rural communities falls even heavier upon remote communities. For example, the term 'remote' does not appear in the aforementioned Cotonou Agreement, which is rather surprising considering that the primary target recipients for aid under the agreement would need to be people in remote locations. Nor does it appear in the UN General Assembly Declaration on the Rights of Peasants and Other People Working in Rural Areas, which is perhaps more understandable considering its terms of reference and objectives. By the same token, academic debate on what constitutes a remote community or its members in the context of non-state actor analysis is remarkably quiet, limited to occasional references in the context of basic services delivery or human rights abuses. On the other hand, remoteness more broadly approached and its relationship with international law has recently been the object of academic inquiry, with Rossi (2021) innovatively discussing the South American desert of Atacama from the intermingled perspectives of historical (colonial) international law, neoliberal extractivism, indigenous rights, water scarcity, and cross-border resource management.

From a physical, spatial perspective, a place "may be remote in several respects: by being at an edge, being far, being ill-connected or by a combination of those" (Bocco 2016, 179). But remote activity and thus some degree of determination of what may constitute a remote community can be influenced by a very broad range of factors—some coterminous and others contradictory. There may be geographical factors of distance or of mountainous terrain, or political factors of distance. There may be cultural, ethnic, attitudinal, or even emotional factors. The geopolitical factors, such as national borders and regional boundaries, are another layer externally imposed on top. Hence, the objectives for seeking and constructing meaningful classifications of 'remote', and for that matter 'rural', are largely driven by specific purposes, such as population census or provision by the state or region of services such as education or health. So, distance from established services or road connectivity seems to become a fairly common determinant. But there still remains enormous diversity in the legal sense in the understanding of what is remoteness and how it may become engaged with in the debate.

While everything that is remote is generally rural in the rural–urban dichotomy, not everything that is rural is necessarily remote. Indeed, writing in the context of the delivery of health services in Canada, Slack, Bourne, and Gertler (2014, 180) state that remoteness is a concept often associated with rurality—and for Canada, with the remote northern region, the "North"—however there is neither complete overlap nor complete separation between rurality and remoteness. The Canadian public health authorities use a taxonomy of "remote" (350 km from the nearest service centre but having year-round road access) and "isolated" communities (no year-round road access). The latter consist, in a large majority, of First Nations, raising complex issues relevant to international law—issues illustrated in the following with the example of another vast country, Australia, where remoteness is even easier to perceive visually in a simple look at the continent's map.

"The North" in Canada has its correspondent in the Australian centre. Specific terminology has emerged in Australia as well: in the "bush" (which might equate, albeit roughly, with rural), a rural property may be measured in hundreds of hectares, but in the "outback" (which would be the equivalent of the Canadian "isolated"), a property may be measured in thousands of square kilometres, and every homestead has a runway and a helicopter or plane as a core form of transport. The associated rural community consists of all those working the property or 'station' and their families.

To illustrate the dimension of remoteness in Australia, the Australian Statistical Geography Standard (ASGS)—a classification of Australia into a hierarchy of statistical areas developed as a social geography to reflect the location of people and communities—is useful. The ASGS includes a Remoteness Areas schedule that divides Australia into five classes of remoteness on the basis of their relative access to services, ranging from Major cities to Inner regional, Outer regional, Remote Australia, and Very remote Australia. Most of Australia's First Nations people live within the Very remote region (49% according to the Australian Institute for Family Studies), and most of Australia's natural resources, wealth, and agricultural regions wealth lie within these regions as well. International law became a tool for neoliberal globalisation and its associated push for resources deep in the heart of First Nations' territory.

This unfortunate (from the First Nations inhabitants' perspective) coexistence is what makes remoteness and its communities uniquely relevant to international law, in what Kleinfeld (2016) has dubbed "the double life of international law". On the one hand, in one of its greatest achievements, international law has provided a special status for indigenous peoples of the world, but on the other hand, keeping pace with technological progress that allowed for exploitation of minerals in places until recently inaccessible, international law has become a tool of neoliberal globalisation. As Kleinfeld (2016) explains:

> [T]he elaboration of legal protections is not the only revolutionary international legal development affecting indigenous wellbeing; globalization and global capitalism have made transnational enterprises influential international actors in their own right, and increasingly so in indigenous spaces. Transnational enterprises have capitalized on monumental opportunities to invest and appropriate surplus value in multiple jurisdictions simultaneously. The proliferation of such opportunities has been facilitated by lowered barriers to foreign trade and investment and supported by national measures and international legal structures, organizations, and instruments—all propelled by once-consensus notions that market liberalization of all types, including capital market liberalization, is a universally preferred economic policy.

A powerful illustration of the complex issues at the intersection of indigeneity, (desertic) remoteness, and colonial juxtaposed on neoliberal greed is presented in the first (to the authors' knowledge) book dealing with remoteness in international law. Using the Atacama desert as a case study and intermingling philosophical, historical, and legal perspectives, Rossi (2021) arrives at similar conclusions regarding the double life of the international law when it comes to First Nations living in remote locations.

But remoteness may also place those communities in a blind spot to domestic law, which in itself invites considerations of the role of international law, at least for those conceiving domestic and international law as a continuum. In the United States, for example, native tribes of Alaska are dramatically impacted by climate change and rising sea levels, yet their remoteness, combined with legislative hurdles, pose significant barriers to state and especially federal assistance (Korkut et al. 2022). In Greece, where vastness takes the form of the myriad of islands scattered around the peninsular part of the country, there are among these islands some that are simply "excluded by the scope of the law" (Nicolini and Perrin 2021, 4).

Remoteness however does not require a huge territory. Papua New Guinea, one of the smallest countries, is home to some of the most remote communities in the world, with around 85% of the population reported to live in rural and/or remote communities. Except for the main coastal population centres in the south and north, road access can be poor between communities, particularly in the monsoon season, and remoteness can be measured in terms of the number of days it can take to travel between two villages 10 kilometres and two mountain ranges apart.

Remoteness can also be sociocultural, created by differing customs and clan groups between communities. Further, remote communities, particularly those that exist in remote areas of a state or are adjacent to or even across national borders, can predate the national borders themselves. They can lose that particular identification as economic factors and population growth cause (urban) spread and consequent overlapping with rural communities. Or a remote community can simply die as its members depart or are even removed through state action for public health reasons or the 'greater good'. A remote community can also lose that original special connotation as newly discovered resources and subsequent mining and developments create large-scale, highly mechanised and industrialised complexes. In such instances the remoteness factor may possibly still remain, but the sense of community and society may be lost.

Given this multitude of facets and dynamics of remote communities, perhaps one measure with which to examine them, and to consider the merits of acknowledging a certain degree of non-state actor status, might be to take into consideration, along with the conventional notions of rural and remote, the *challenges* that the community is facing. Following are a few examples of specific challenges encountered by remote communities, some of which are already being confronted by both state actors and non-state actors:

- Remote communities adversely impacted by the effects of climate change because of global warming, such as the Northwest Arctic village of Kivalina, which was one of the complainants in the complaint to the UN mentioned in the Introduction of this book. Their tragic case adds to those of small island communities of the Indo-Pacific states subject to rising sea levels washing away their coastlines. Other climate impacts on rural communities include devastation by years of drought in Africa, and by rainfall and flooding in the Indian sub-continent.
- Remote communities witnessing destruction and degradation of their natural environment and ecosystems for wealth generation and industrial development. As remote locations are less visible to authorities and the public opinion, places such as the jungles and forests of the Amazon basin region have long been subject to clearing for mining and industrial and agricultural development. Similarly, the forests of Indonesia have been

subject to clearing through burning for palm oil plantations, generating air pollution and health hazard throughout the region.
- Remote communities having their way of life and very existence drastically and directly impacted by the operations of major national or international corporations, some of which may be conducted with state approval or contrary to state regulation. For example, Ecuador has been engaged in ongoing litigation and arbitration against Chevron Oil before international tribunals and Dutch and US courts since the 1990s over Chevron's oil exploration and production operations in Ecuador's Amazon basin region in the north of the country. The claims have included destruction of indigenous communities and wholesale pollution of waterways.
- Unregulated fracking for oil extraction and water extraction either unlicenced or unregulated or without prior scientific impact research, and consequent impact on artesian resources and water tables, affecting remote communities in particular.
- Indigenous and First Nations people whose ownership and connections to their lands by custom and tradition have been, and continue to be, challenged by state actors and multinational corporations.
- Nomadic communities, particularly those who travel across borders between under-developed or non-developed regions of states, such as the Bedu of the Arabian Gulf, and those who cross as a matter of practice and identity and who may be seen as a material and ideational threat, such as the Sami of Norway, Sweden, and Finland and the Romanis of Europe.
- Remote communities which become targets for or collaborate with international terrorist and armed insurgent groups who perceive the community, because of their remoteness as an operational base, a supply chain component, a source of income or even as a recruitment source. For example, the recruitment of child soldiers by a number of terrorist groups in Mali, Sudan, Democratic Republic of the Congo, and other African states and a wide range of activities carried out by al-Qaeda and ISIS.
- Remote communities collaborating with transnational organised crime groups and drug cartels, sometimes under threat or as a source of income, and sometimes dealing with both human victims and/or material/products. For example, acting as couriers across borders, or primary producers of narcotics within the "golden crescent of" Afghanistan/Pakistan/Iran and the "golden triangle" of Thailand/Laos/Myanmar.
- Remote communities who have become victims of persecution and alleged genocide by state actors, such as the Rohingya people of northern Myanmar. The persecution of the Rohingya people appears to have worsen further since the military coup in Myanmar in early 2021, leading to the involvement of a host of humanitarian and development organisations as non-state actors. This epitomises their role in circumstances requiring the application of international law principles and practices to the benefit of those whose needs and rights have not been—often, because of their

community's remoteness—acknowledged or addressed adequately by their state.
- Remote communities in outlying islands of archipelagic states, who have become embroiled in maritime boundary territorial disputes between states' actors, such as the ongoing South China Sea disputation between China and particularly the Philippines (but also Vietnam and Indonesia), and its creation of man-made islands as boundary markers to justify its claims.

These challenges are within the remit and responsibility of the state actor to address, but remoteness poses subjective and objective challenges to its capacity to act properly in the interest of the remote community. Subjectively, the state may simply not be interested in expanding resources into an isolated community that brings only a handful of votes. Objectively, communicational and logistic hurdles may impede action in favour of remote communities, including remote communities confronted with transnational risks, such as those victims to paramilitary cross-border groups in weak states. Remoteness therefore invites considerations on the relevance of international law to fill these spaces. In other words, the remote community can (or should) become, when necessary, one of those spaces referred to in the critical geography literature as the "unlikeliest of places" where international law can exist (Pearson 2008, referring to the city as such unlikely space, but admitting that there can be non-urban spaces 'inhabited' by international law as well).

With the overview of remote communities' relevance to international law developed in the present section, this chapter hopefully establishes the merits of the recognition or acknowledgement of rural communities, including remote communities, as non-state actors. The extension from rural to remote communities was based on the observation that, depending on the physical, political, social, and geographical factors, many rural and remote communities have similar or even common or related aspirations and needs. In doing this extension, this chapter has endeavoured to promote the cause of both rural and remote communities as participants, willing or otherwise, in the arenas in which non-state actors exist and operate.

References

Alvik, Ivan. 2020. "The Justification of Privilege in International Investment Law: Preferential Treatment of Foreign Investors as a Problem of Legitimacy." *European Journal of International Law* 31 (1): 289–312.

Aust, Helmut P., and Janne E. Nijman, eds. 2021. *Research Handbook on International Law and Cities*. Cheltenham: Edward Elgar.

Besson, Samantha, and José Luis Martí. 2021. "Democratic Representatives in International Law-Making." In *Research Handbook on International Law and Cities*, edited by Helmut P. Aust and Janne E. Nijman, 341–53. Cheltenham: Edward Elgar.

Bocco, Gerardo. 2016. "Remoteness and Remote Places: A Geographic Perspective." *Geoforum* 77: 178–81.
Brumann, Christoph. 2015. "Community as Myth and Reality in the UNESCO World Heritage Convention." In *Between Imagined Communities and Communities of Practice: Participation, Territory, and the Making of Heritage*, edited by Nicolas Adell, Regina F. Bendix, Chiara Bortolatto, and Markus Tauschek, 273–90. Göttingen: Göttingen University Press.
Cotula, Lorenzo. 2022. "The Right to Land." In *The United Nations' Declaration on Peasants' Rights*, edited by Mariagrazia Alabrese, Adriana Bessa, Marherita Brunori, and Pier Filippo Giuggioli, 91–105. Abingdon and New York: Routledge.
D'Aspremont, Jean. 2011. "Non-State Actors from the Perspective of Legal Positivism: The Communitarian Semantics for the Secondary Rules of International Life." In *Participants in the International Legal System: Multiple Perspectives on Non-State Actors in International Law*, edited by Jean d'Aspremont, 23–40. Abingdon and New York: Routledge.
———. 2012. "Reductionist Legal Positivism in International Law." *ASIL Proceedings* 106 (1): 368–70.
Falk, Richard A. 1995. "Casting the Spell: The New Haven School of International Law." *Yale Journal of International Law* 104 (7): 1991–2008.
Fassbender, Bardo. 1998. "The United Nations Constitution of the International Community." *Columbia Journal of Transnational Law* 36 (3): 529–620.
Gibbs, Melissa, Alex Gooding, Ronald Woods, Stefanie Pillora, and Ryan Smith. 2015. *Sister Cities and International Alliances*. Sydney: Australian Centre of Excellence for Local Government.
Hathaway, Oona A. 2007. "The Continuing Influence of the New Haven School." *Yale Journal of International Law* 32 (2): 553–58.
Holmes, Oliver W. 1897. "The Path of the Law." *Harvard Law Review* 10 (8): 457–78.
International Law Association (ILA). 2016. "Final Report on Non-State Actors." Johannesburg Conference.
Klabbers, Jan. 2019. "International Constitutionalism." In *The Cambridge Companion to Comparative Constitutional Law*, edited by Robert Masterman and Robert Schütze, 498–520. Cambridge and New York: Cambridge University Press.
Klabbers, Jan, Anne Peters, and Geir Ulfstein. 2009. *The Constitutionalization of International Law*. New York: Oxford University Press.
Kleinfeld, Joshua. 2016. "The Double Life of International Law: Indigenous Peoples and Extractive Industries." *Harvard Law Review* 129 (6): 1755. https://harvardlawreview.org/2016/04/the-double-life-of-international-law-indigenous-peoples-and-extractive-industries/.
Kleinlein, Thomas. 2011. "Non-State Actors from an International Constitutionalist Perspective: Participation Matters!" In *Participants in the International Legal System—Multiple Perspectives on Non-State Actors in International Law*, edited by Jean D'Aspremont, 41–53. Abingdon and New York: Routledge.
———. 2012. "Between Myths and Norms: Constructivist Constitutionalism and the Potential of Constitutional Principles in International Law." *Nordic Journal of International Law* 81 (1): 79–132.
Koh, Harold H. 2007. "Is There a 'New' New Haven School of International Law?" *Yale Journal of International Law* 32 (2): 559–74.
Kolb, Robert. 2016. *Theory of International Law*. Portland: Hart Publishing.

Korkut, Ekrem, Lara B. Fowler, Kathleen E. Halvorsen, Davin Holen, E. Lance Howe, and Guangqing Chi. 2022. "Addressing Climate Impacts in Alaska Native Tribes." *UCLA Journal of Environmental Law and Policy* 40 (2): 185–228.

Krisch, N. 2010. *Beyond Constitutionalism: The Pluralist Structure of Postnational Law*. Oxford: Oxford University Press.

Lasswell, Harold D., and Myres S. McDougal. 1943. "Legal Education and Public Policy: Professional Training in the Public Interest." *Yale Law Journal* 52 (2): 203–95.

Levit, Janet K. 2007. "Bottom-Up International Lawmaking: Reflections on the New Haven School of International Law." *Yale Journal of International Law* 32 (2): 393–420.

McDougal, Myres S. 1953. "International Law, Power and Policy: A Contemporary Conception." *The Hague Academy of International Law* 82: 137–258.

———. 1960. "Some Basic Theoretical Concepts about International Law: A Policy-Oriented Framework of Inquiry." *Journal of Conflict Resolution* 4 (3): 337–54.

Nicolini, Matteo, and Thomas Perrin. 2021. "Geographical Connections: Law, Islands, and Remoteness." *Liverpool Law Review* 42 (1): 1–14.

Onuf, Nicholas G. 1982. "Global Law-Making and Legal Thought." In *Law-Making in the Global Community*, edited by Nicholas G. Onuf, 1–81. Durham, NC: Carolina Academic Press.

Pearson, Zoe. 2008. "Spaces of International Law." *Griffith Law Review* 17 (2): 489–514.

Peters, Anne. 2009. "The Merits of Global Constitutionalism." *Indiana Journal of Global Legal Studies* 16 (2): 397–411.

Reisman, Michael W. 1992. "The View from the New Haven School of International Law." *ASIL Proceedings* 86: 118–24.

Reisman, Michael W., Siegfried Wiessner, and Andrew R. Willard. 2007. "The New Haven School: A Brief Introduction." *Yale Journal of International Law* 32 (2): 575–82.

Rodiles, Alejandro. 2021. "The Global Insecure Counterterrorism City." In *Research Handbook on International Law and Cities*, edited by Helmut P. Aust and Janne E. Nijman, 214–26. Cheltenham: Edward Elgar.

Rossi, Christopher R. 2021. *Remoteness Reconsidered: The Atacama Desert and International Law*. Ann Arbor: University of Michigan Press.

Schachter, Oscar. 1985. "McDougal's Jurisprudence: Utility, Influence, Controversy." *ASIL Proceedings* 79: 266–73.

Slack, Enid, Larry S. Bourne, and Meric S. Gertler. 2003. "Small, Rural, and Remote Communities: The Anatomy of Risk." A paper prepared for the Panel on the Role of Government. Toronto, Canada (13 August).

Suzuki, Eisuke. 1974. "The New Haven School of International Law: An Invitation to a Policy-Oriented Jurisprudence." *Yale Studies in World Public Order*: 1–48.

Tomuschat, Christian. 1999. *International Law: Ensuring the Survival of Mankind on the Eve of a New Century: General Course on Public International Law*. Leiden: Martinus Nijhoff.

UN Habitat. 2018. "Cities Are Engines for Achieving the Sustainable Development Goals." UN Press Release, July 17. https://unhabitat.org/cities-are-engines-for-achieving-the-sustainable-development-goals.

UNSC Committee Chair. 2019. Letter from the Chair of the Security Council Committee Established Pursuant to Resolution 1373 (2001) Concerning Counter-Terrorism Addressed to the President of the Security Council. Annex, UN Doc. S/2019/998, December 27, 2019.

Urbinati, Sabrina. 2015. "The Community Participation in International Law." In *Between Imagined Communities and Communities of Practice: Participation, Territory, and the Making of Heritage*, edited by Nicolas Adell, Regina F. Bendix, Chiara Bortolatto, and Markus Tauschek, 123–40. Göttingen: Göttingen University Press.

Waters, Melissa A. 2007. "Normativity in the 'New' Schools: Assessing the Legitimacy of International Legal Norms Created by Domestic Courts." *Yale Journal of International Law* 32 (2): 455–84.

Cases

Bear Creek Mining Corp. v. Republic of Peru, ICSID Case No. ARB/14/21, Award § 738 (November 30, 2017).

Chandler v. Cape plc [2012] EWCA Civ. 525 (Eng. & Wales).

Choc v. Hudbay Minerals (2013) ONSC 1414 (Can.).

Lungowe and Others v. Vedanta Res. PLC and Konkola Copper Mines PLC [2017] EWCA Civ 1528.

Lupaka Gold Corp. v. Republic of Peru, ICSID Case No. ARB/20/46, Expert Report of Accuracy §1 (October 1, 2021).

Vito G. Gallo v. Government of Canada, PCA Case No. 55798, NAFTA/UNCITRAL, 18 (Perm. Ct. Arb. 2011).

Conclusion

The aim of this book is to remove the "veil of invisibility" that surrounds non-urban communities when it comes to international law. Chapter 1 examined the matter from the perspective of non-state actors generally: is there space in the definitional sphere of the concept for the rural and remote communities? The analysis suggested a cautious 'yes'. Indeed, pleading the cause of rural and remote communities as non-state actors has been facilitated by definitional uncertainty regarding the latter: inbuilt uncertainty, but also uncertainty stemming from recent dynamics.

The fundamental question on what may constitute a non-state actor continues to be engaged by commentators and scholars, as Philip Alston's oft-quoted "not-a-cat" syndrome (2005b, 3–4) offered almost two decades ago is still as relevant today. Criticising the categorisation of the term 'non-state actor' by what it does *not* refer to (the state), Alston (2005b, 7) also notes that using a term such as non-state actors risks transforming the analysis of very concrete issues into a purely academic exercise, detached from the sometimes harsh realities and often very practical dilemmas that arise. Mindful of such risk, the authors acknowledge that a certain degree of cautious reflection is needed to avoid an overenthusiastic approach to an ongoing extension of non-state actor categorisation.

Yet the truth remains that first, there is no generally accepted definition of the term 'non-state actor' in international law, and second, such is the pace of change in international dynamics that even if there was a definition a few decades ago, it could be challenged today. When an august and active body such as the European Commission (2002, 5) explains in its report to the European Parliament on the participation of non-state actors in EC development policy that non-state actors are created by citizens "to promote an issue or an interest, either general or specific" and can be either operators or advocates, this generous definition arguably creates a space for the inclusion of entities such as the rural and remote communities.

Chapter 2 espoused a cause for recognition, or at least case-based acknowledgement, of rural communities and remote communities as non-state actors on the grounds that they can display the essential participatory characteristics

DOI: 10.4324/9781003385318-4

Conclusion

required to be regarded as such in terms of their treaty recognition and/or their accumulative capacity to influence international decision-making and equitable rights in national and transnational decision-making impacting on them. Starting with rural communities, Chapter 2 shows that they display enough of the characteristics required to be regarded as non-state actors. The examination proceeded from three perspectives, each built on one of the grand theories of international law: participation as stipulated in treaties (a positivist perspective); participation as a fact when the rural community accumulates the power to influence international decision-making (a sociologist/realist perspective); and participation as a matter of fairness and justice in decisions that impact upon the rural community (a natural law perspective).

If there is a veil of invisibility drawn in respect of rural communities in international law, then this assertion applies with equal or more weight in relation to remote communities, since some transnational governance areas can concern remote communities exclusively, as shown in Chapter 2, 'Taking the Argument Further: Remote Communities in International Law'. Therefore, if there is merit in acknowledging rural commodities as non-state actors when issues such as those challenging their fundamental human rights or their way of life or even their existence arise, then a similar proposition in respect of remote communities has similar merit.

The extension from rural to remote communities in Chapter 2, 'Taking the Argument Further: Remote Communities in International Law' is an example of the continuous expansion of the boundaries of the non-state actor concept, noted by the International Law Association in their final report on the matter: "Through the procedures of formal incorporation and informal integration, [international law] has taken account of the rise of non-state actors. Its response, however, has not been comprehensive or systematic but, rather, incremental and on a case-by-case basis." The analysis of rural and remote communities is offered as an example of this creeping semantic development, but where does this lead, in terms of the concept's relevance? Is there a risk of taking the 'non-state actor' concept on a road to nowhere— repeating the story of 'sustainability', a concept which, when expanded from environmental sustainability to integrate social concerns and economic interests, lost much of its practical relevance (e.g., Beckerman 1994; Hickel 2019)? Paraphrasing the title of a critique of sustainable development as an excessively broad concept (Farley and Smith 2013), if a non-state actor is everything, is it nothing? Even though the rural and remote communities as non-state actors was facilitated by the unsettled boundaries of the non-state actor concept, there is still need for caution in venturing too far within the current theoretical regimes of international law in endeavouring to expand the membership qualifications. Further debate on the role of rural and remote in international law will hopefully tell whether the hypothesis and argument presented here are valid.

Even if logic and academic rigour will challenge this book's contention, there is a moral angle to it which, it is suggested, can hardly be dismissed or ignored. Rural, remote, and especially poor communities are already relevant to international law, but in an oppressive manner—they are silenced and abused, as noted in the academic literature:

> [F]undamental components of international law systematically obstruct the aspirations of poor populations for democratic self-government, civil rights, and minimal economic sufficiency. And central international organizations, like the World Trade Organization (WTO), the International Monetary Fund (IMF), and the World Bank, are designed so that they systematically contribute to the persistence of severe poverty.
> (Pogge 2005, 717)

Our contention is that they have, or should have, a voice. In his rejoinder to Professor Thirlway on non-state actors in international law, Ryngaert (2017, 160) quotes and analyses two lines offered to him by Thirlway from T S Eliot's *The Lovesong of J. Alfred Prufrock*: "No! I am not Prince Hamlet, nor was meant to be; Am an attendant lord". Professor Ryngaert suggests that the lines could be interpreted, when applied by analogy to non-state actors, as non-state actors acquiescing in their destiny as secondary actors on the world stage in the shadow of the society of states.

The temptation to extend Ryngaert's movie world analogy is overwhelming: what this book has endeavoured to achieve is an examination of whether the rural community has turned from an extra (actors with minor appearance in the film, without any line of dialogue—perhaps a Ukrainian village exporting grains to Africa) to a supporting actor (those with lines in the film—again, perhaps a Ukrainian village assisting the army with information on the movements of the invader's troops). Whether from a descriptive perspective the intellectual edifice built here stands or not may be a matter of debate. But from a prescriptive perspective, the global half of the population living in rural and remote areas should have its place under the sun of the international law, with the limitations acknowledged throughout this book.

References

Alston, Philippe. 2005b. "The 'Not-a-Cat' Syndrome: Can the International Human Rights Regime Accommodate Non-State Actors?" In *Non-State Actors and Human Rights*, edited by Philippe Alston, 3–36. Oxford: Oxford University Press.

Beckerman, Wilfred. 1994. "Sustainable Development: Is It a Useful Concept?" *Environmental Values* 3 (3): 191–209.

European Commission. 2002. Communication from the Commission to the Council, the European Parliament and the Economic and Social Committee: Participation of Non-State Actors in EC Development Policy. COM (2002) 598 final.

Farley, Heather M., and Zachary A. Smith. 2013. *Sustainability: If It's Everything, Is It Nothing?* New York: Routledge.
Hickel, Jason. 2019. "The Contradiction of the Sustainable Development Goals: Growth Versus Ecology on a Finite Planet." *Sustainable Development* 27 (5): 873–84.
Pogge, Thomas. 2005. "Recognized and Violated by International Law: The Human Rights of the Global Poor." *Leiden Journal of International Law* 18 (4): 717–45.
Ryngaert, Cedric. 2017. "Non-State Actors in International Law: A Rejoinder to Professor Thirlway." *Netherlands International Law Review* 64 (1): 155–62.